Using Addition Facts Through 18

Add.

1. 6 +5	**2.** 7 +7	**3.** 8 +3	**4.** 8 +8	**5.** 6 +7
6. 5 +8	**7.** 6 +6	**8.** 7 +8	**9.** 9 +4	**10.** 9 +9
11. 9 +0	**12.** 8 +6	**13.** 5 +7	**14.** 9 +8	**15.** 0 +2

16. $7 + 6 =$ _____   **17.** $9 + 6 =$ _____   **18.** $4 + 8 =$ _____

19. $9 + 5 =$ _____   **20.** $1 + 6 =$ _____   **21.** $4 + 5 =$ _____

Find the output.

Rule: Add 9.

	Input	Output
22.	3	
23.	7	
24.	5	
25.	8	

Rule: Add 3.

	Input	Output
26.	12	
27.	6	
28.	4	
29.	9	

Solve.

30. Molly and Pam each made 4 potholders. How many potholders did they make altogether?

_____

Adding Three Numbers

Add.

1.	3 2 +6	2.	7 0 +4	3.	5 4 +4	4.	4 1 +8	5.	5 4 +3

6.	7 2 +7	7.	7 1 +8	8.	6 1 +7	9.	8 0 +9	10.	2 3 +4

11.	5 0 +8	12.	4 4 +4	13.	2 2 +7	14.	1 0 +8	15.	7 2 +6

16. $6 + 0 + 9 = \underline{}$ 17. $7 + 1 + 6 = \underline{}$ 18. $4 + 4 + 3 = \underline{}$

19. $7 + 2 + 3 = \underline{}$ 20. $5 + 4 + 0 = \underline{}$ 21. $3 + 1 + 8 = \underline{}$

Choose the correct sum. Circle the letter of your answer.

22. $6 + 3 + 4 = \boxed{}$ a. 13   b. 12   c. 14

23. $5 + 0 + 6 = \boxed{}$ a. 5   b. 16   c. 11

24. $4 + 5 + 2 = \boxed{}$ a. 10   b. 11   c. 12

Mixed Review

Add.

1.	5 +4	2.	8 +1	3.	3 +7	4.	4 +3	5.	2 +8	6.	6 +3

7.	7 +1	8.	3 +6	9.	2 +6	10.	7 +5	11.	6 +3	12.	8 +3

Problem-Solving Strategies: Finding Facts from Pictures

Use the picture to answer each question.

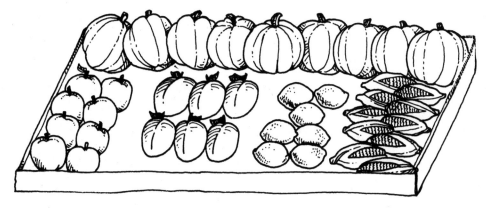

1. How many apples are there? _____

2. How many peaches are there? _____

3. How many lemons are there? _____

4. How many pumpkins and peaches are
   there? _____

5. How many lemons and peaches are there? _____

6. Are there more lemons or apples? _____

7. Mark bought 4 pumpkins. How many
   pumpkins are left? _____

8. Jennifer bought 4 ears of corn. Barry
   bought the same amount of corn as
   Jennifer. How many ears of corn did Barry
   buy? _____

9. Carl needs 8 lemons to make lemonade.
   Are there enough lemons at the farm
   stand? _____

10. If Tracy buys 4 apples, will Mark be able to
    buy 5 apples? Explain.

_____

Relating Addition and Subtraction Facts

Find each missing addend. Then write each difference.

1.
$$\begin{array}{r} 7 \\ +\ \square \\ \hline 11 \end{array} \qquad \begin{array}{r} 11 \\ -\ 7 \\ \hline \end{array}$$

2.
$$\begin{array}{r} 9 \\ +\ \square \\ \hline 18 \end{array} \qquad \begin{array}{r} 18 \\ -\ 9 \\ \hline \end{array}$$

3.
$$\begin{array}{r} 6 \\ +\ \square \\ \hline 9 \end{array} \qquad \begin{array}{r} 9 \\ -6 \\ \hline \end{array}$$

4.
$$\begin{array}{r} 4 \\ +\ \square \\ \hline 12 \end{array} \qquad \begin{array}{r} 12 \\ -\ 4 \\ \hline \end{array}$$

5.
$$\begin{array}{r} 8 \\ +\ \square \\ \hline 17 \end{array} \qquad \begin{array}{r} 17 \\ -\ 8 \\ \hline \end{array}$$

6.
$$\begin{array}{r} 6 \\ +\ \square \\ \hline 7 \end{array} \qquad \begin{array}{r} 7 \\ -6 \\ \hline \end{array}$$

7.
$$\begin{array}{r} 5 \\ +\ \square \\ \hline 11 \end{array} \qquad \begin{array}{r} 11 \\ -\ 5 \\ \hline \end{array}$$

8.
$$\begin{array}{r} 5 \\ +\ \square \\ \hline 13 \end{array} \qquad \begin{array}{r} 13 \\ -\ 5 \\ \hline \end{array}$$

9. $9 + \square = 13$

   $13 - 9 = \underline{\hphantom{000}}$

10. $6 + \square = 10$

   $10 - 6 = \underline{\hphantom{000}}$

11. $6 + \square = 12$

   $12 - 6 = \underline{\hphantom{000}}$

12. $4 + \square = 13$

   $13 - 4 = \underline{\hphantom{000}}$

Mixed Review

Add or subtract.

1. $\begin{array}{r} 3 \\ +4 \\ \hline \end{array}$ **2.** $\begin{array}{r} 4 \\ +4 \\ \hline \end{array}$ **3.** $\begin{array}{r} 3 \\ +7 \\ \hline \end{array}$ **4.** $\begin{array}{r} 5 \\ +0 \\ \hline \end{array}$ **5.** $\begin{array}{r} 8 \\ +2 \\ \hline \end{array}$ **6.** $\begin{array}{r} 7 \\ +1 \\ \hline \end{array}$

7. $\begin{array}{r} 7 \\ -1 \\ \hline \end{array}$ **8.** $\begin{array}{r} 10 \\ -\ 2 \\ \hline \end{array}$ **9.** $\begin{array}{r} 5 \\ -1 \\ \hline \end{array}$ **10.** $\begin{array}{r} 9 \\ -6 \\ \hline \end{array}$ **11.** $\begin{array}{r} 9 \\ -2 \\ \hline \end{array}$ **12.** $\begin{array}{r} 6 \\ -4 \\ \hline \end{array}$

Using Subtraction Facts Through 18

Subtract.

1. 15 − 7	2. 9 − 0	3. 14 − 7	4. 15 − 9	5. 14 − 6

6. 17 − 9	7. 6 − 6	8. 13 − 4	9. 16 − 8	10. 14 − 5

11. 18 − 9	12. 15 − 8	13. 16 − 9	14. 14 − 9	15. 8 − 8

16. $14 - 8 =$ _____ 17. $7 - 7 =$ _____ 18. $13 - 4 =$ _____

19. $15 - 7 =$ _____ 20. $17 - 8 =$ _____ 21. $12 - 8 =$ _____

22. $12 - 3 =$ _____ 23. $13 - 7 =$ _____ 24. $4 - 4 =$ _____

Solve.

25. There are 15 books and 8 children. How
    many more books are there than children.   _____ books

≡ Mixed Review ≡

◆ Add or subtract. Use mental math or paper and pencil.

1. 3 1 +1	2. 4 2 +3	3. 3 0 +3	4. 4 1 +5	5. 2 1 +3	6. 2 0 +1

7. 10 − 4	8. 9 − 2	9. 9 − 8	10. 8 − 3	11. 10 − 3	12. 10 − 5

13. $7 - 1 =$ _____ 14. $12 - 3 =$ _____ 15. $9 - 5 =$ _____

16. $8 - 6 =$ _____ 17. $7 + 7 =$ _____ 18. $12 + 6 =$ _____

Use with text pages 18–19.

Using Fact Families

Complete each fact family.

1. 8 + 7 = _____

7 + 8 = _____

15 − 7 = _____

15 − 8 = _____

2. 6 + 8 = _____

8 + 6 = _____

14 − 6 = _____

14 − 8 = _____

3. 9 + 7 = _____

7 + 9 = _____

16 − 7 = _____

16 − 9 = _____

4. 9 + 3 = _____

3 + 9 = _____

12 − 3 = _____

12 − 9 = _____

5. 7 + 6 = _____

6 + 7 = _____

13 − 6 = _____

13 − 7 = _____

6. 5 + 9 = _____

9 + 5 = _____

14 − 5 = _____

14 − 9 = _____

Write a fact family for each.

7. | 4, 5, 9 |

8. | 8, 4, 12 |

_____ _____   _____ _____

_____ _____   _____ _____

Mixed Review

Add or subtract.

1. 7 + 6 = _____

2. 5 + 8 = _____

3. 6 + 9 = _____

4. 11 − 2 = _____

5. 15 − 9 = _____

6. 12 − 6 = _____

Compare. Write >, <, or = in each ◯ .

7. 8 + 2 ◯ 11 − 1

8. 6 + 7 ◯ 4 + 8

9. 15 − 4 ◯ 5 + 7

10. 16 − 6 ◯ 7 + 4

Use with text pages 20–21.

Using Problems Solving: Odd or Even?

Write three facts for each.
Then write *even* or *odd* to make each
statement correct.

1. **ODD + ODD**

_____ + _____ = _____

_____ + _____ = _____

_____ + _____ = _____

The sums are _____.

2. **EVEN + EVEN**

_____ + _____ = _____

_____ + _____ = _____

_____ + _____ = _____

The sums are _____.

3. **ODD + EVEN**

_____ + _____ = _____

_____ + _____ = _____

_____ + _____ = _____

The sums are _____.

4. **ODD − EVEN**

_____ − _____ = _____

_____ − _____ = _____

_____ − _____ = _____

The differences are _____.

5. **EVEN − EVEN**

_____ − _____ = _____

_____ − _____ = _____

_____ − _____ = _____

The differences are _____.

6. **ODD − ODD**

_____ − _____ = _____

_____ − _____ = _____

_____ − _____ = _____

The differences are _____.

Mixed Review

Add or subtract.

1. $9 - 8 =$ ___

2. $4 + 4 =$ ___

3. $12 - 6 =$ ___

4. $4 + 3 =$ ___

5. $8 + 7 =$ ___

6. $14 - 6 =$ ___

Reading and Writing Whole Numbers

Write each number.

1.

2.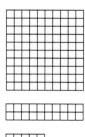

_____

_____

3. 5 tens 2 ones _____

4. 9 tens 8 ones _____

5. 3 hundreds 4 tens 0 ones

6. 6 hundreds 2 tens 3 ones

_____

_____

7. $20 + 5 =$ _____

8. $70 + 4 =$ _____

9. $500 + 80 + 9 =$ _____

10. $800 + 20 + 6 =$ _____

Write the word name for each number.

11. 68

12. 211

_____

_____

Mixed Review

Add or subtract.

1. $\begin{array}{r} 6 \\ +3 \\ \hline \end{array}$	2. $\begin{array}{r} 2 \\ +4 \\ \hline \end{array}$	3. $\begin{array}{r} 7 \\ +0 \\ \hline \end{array}$	4. $\begin{array}{r} 4 \\ +4 \\ \hline \end{array}$	5. $\begin{array}{r} 5 \\ +4 \\ \hline \end{array}$	6. $\begin{array}{r} 2 \\ +3 \\ \hline \end{array}$
7. $\begin{array}{r} 2 \\ +5 \\ \hline \end{array}$	8. $\begin{array}{r} 3 \\ +5 \\ \hline \end{array}$	9. $\begin{array}{r} 3 \\ +3 \\ \hline \end{array}$	10. $\begin{array}{r} 10 \\ -5 \\ \hline \end{array}$	11. $\begin{array}{r} 8 \\ -3 \\ \hline \end{array}$	12. $\begin{array}{r} 5 \\ -1 \\ \hline \end{array}$
13. $\begin{array}{r} 6 \\ -0 \\ \hline \end{array}$	14. $\begin{array}{r} 5 \\ -4 \\ \hline \end{array}$	15. $\begin{array}{r} 9 \\ -2 \\ \hline \end{array}$	16. $\begin{array}{r} 8 \\ -2 \\ \hline \end{array}$	17. $\begin{array}{r} 6 \\ -2 \\ \hline \end{array}$	18. $\begin{array}{r} 10 \\ -2 \\ \hline \end{array}$

Using Ordinals

Use the pattern to find the missing numbers.

1. 50, 60, 70, _____, _____, _____

2. 310, 410, 510, _____, _____, _____

3. 35, 45, _____, 65, _____, _____

4. 200, _____, _____, 500, 600, _____

5. 120, _____, 130, 135, _____, _____

6. 315, 325, _____, _____, 355, _____

7. 55, 60, 65, _____, _____, _____

SCIENCE CAMP
1. Nell Jones
2. Agnes Moore
3. Bob Camp
4. Jose Torres
5. Alice Schulty
6. Linda Huss

Nell Jones was the first person to sign up for science camp. Name the person who signed up in each position.

8. two after third

_____

9. one before fourth

_____

10. three after first

_____

11. one after fifth

_____

Mixed Review

Add or subtract.

1.	2.	3.	4.	5.	6.
4	8	3	4	8	8
+3	+1	+3	+3	+2	−3

7.	8.	9.	10.	11.	12.
7	8	7	6	4	8
+1	−8	−5	−3	+2	−1

Rounding to the Nearest Ten or Hundred

Round to the nearest ten.

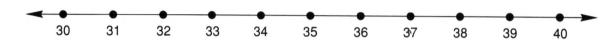

1. 32 ____ 2. 35 ____ 3. 38 ____ 4. 34 ____ 5. 36 ____ 6. 31 ____

7. 45 ____ 8. 53 ____ 9. 71 ____ 10. 89 ____ 11. 24 ____ 12. 67 ____

Round to the nearest ten. Circle the letter
of the correct answer.

13. 57
   a. 50
   b. 60
   c. 70

14. 41
   a. 30
   b. 40
   c. 50

15. 75
   a. 50
   b. 70
   c. 80

16. 92
   a. 80
   b. 90
   b. 100

Round to the nearest hundred.

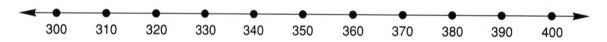

17. 341 _____ 18. 350 _____ 19. 363 _____ 20. 329 _____

21. 435 _____ 22. 529 _____ 23. 617 _____ 24. 903 _____

25. 173 _____ 26. 444 _____ 27. 681 _____ 28. 550 _____

Mixed Review

Add or subtract.

1.	2.	3.	4.	5.	6.
3	5	6	4	8	5
4	3	1	2	1	4
+4	+5	+8	+7	+1	+3

7.	8.	9.	10.	11.	12.
14	11	16	18	16	12
− 2	− 6	− 2	− 9	− 8	− 5

Writing Whole Numbers Through Thousands

Write each number.

1. 2 thousands 4 hundreds 2 tens 5 ones _____

2. 6 thousands 1 hundred 0 tens 9 ones _____

3. 8 thousands 3 hundreds 4 tens 2 ones _____

4. 5 thousands 6 hundreds 9 tens 4 ones _____

5. 5,000 + 600 + 70 + 9 _____   6. 9,000 + 800 + 20 + 1 _____

7. 1,000 + 200 + 4 _____   8. 4,000 + 200 + 50 + 7 _____

Give the value of the digit 5.

9. 4,563   10. 5,014   11. 1,250   12. 6,745

_____   _____   _____   _____

Write the word name for each.

13. 275 _____

14. 3,407 _____

15. 8,015 _____

Mixed Review

Add.

1. 5	2. 3	3. 2	4. 9	5. 3	6. 4
+2	+3	+8	+0	+7	+3

Write the numbers that come between.

7. 16 and 19   8. 27 and 32   9. 49 and 55

_____   _____   _____

Use with text pages 44–45.

Problem-Solving Strategies: Experiment

Trace as many figures as needed to answer
each question.

1. How many circles will fit inside the square?

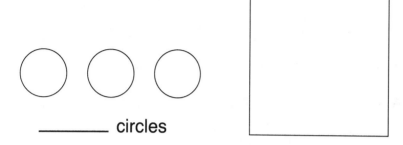

_____ circles

2. How many big paper clips will go around the
picture?

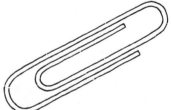

_____ paper clips

3. How many little paper clips will go around
the picture?

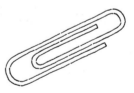

_____ paper clips

Mixed Strategy Review

Solve by using problem-solving strategies.

Tony, Pete, and Andrew are playing marbles.
Can each boy have the same number of
marbles?

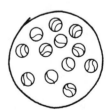

_____

Comparing and Ordering Whole Numbers

Compare. Write > or < in each ◯.

1. 322 ◯ 321

2. 689 ◯ 3,869

3. 5,018 ◯ 5,118

4. 870 ◯ 6,087

5. 8,432 ◯ 4,823

6. 581 ◯ 381

7. 4,960 ◯ 4,962

8. 9,180 ◯ 8,190

9. 2,224 ◯ 2,325

Write the numbers in order from least to greatest.

10. 3,246   2,436   4,233

_____ _____ _____

11. 6,198   3,427   7,866

_____ _____ _____

12. 4,380   4,038   3,444

_____ _____ _____

13. 1,326   3,621   6,140

_____ _____ _____

14. 999   9   9,000

_____ _____ _____

15. 4,022   8,042   2,048

_____ _____ _____

16. 77   7   7,777

_____ _____ _____

17. 3,906   9,063   6,039

_____ _____ _____

Mixed Review

Add or subtract.

1. 8
   +9

2. 7
   +5

3. 8
   +8

4. 4
   +9

5. 2
   +9

6. 8
   +4

7. 13
   − 5

8. 12
   − 4

9. 11
   − 7

10. 11
    − 3

11. 13
    − 7

12. 12
    − 9

13. 9 + 8 = _____

14. 5 + 9 = _____

15. 8 + 4 = _____

16. 11 − 6 = _____

17. 13 − 9 = _____

18. 12 − 7 = _____

Use with text pages 48–49.

Writing Ten-Thousands and Hundred-Thousands

Write the value of the digit 6.

1. 3, 619, 125 _____

2. 1, 463, 112 _____

3. 84, 261, 247 _____

Write each number.

4. 16 thousands, 4 hundreds, 7 tens, 2 ones   _____

5. 453 thousands, 1 hundreds, 6 tens, 3 ones   _____

6. one hundred five thousand, six hundred ten   _____

7. 80,000 + 2,000 + 300 + 70 + 2   _____

8. 400,000 + 7,000 + 9   _____

9. 10,000 + 9,000 + 400 + 20   _____

Write the word name.

10. 520,007 _____

Mixed Review

Add or subtract.

1.	2.	3.	4.	5.	6.
3	2	2	6	3	4
3	1	4	0	3	3
+0	+2	+1	+2	+3	+1

7.	8.	9.	10.	11.	12.
11	14	15	12	11	14
− 8	− 5	− 7	− 9	− 5	− 7

Finding Values of Money to $10.00

Write each value. Use a dollar sign and a decimal point.

1. forty-two cents _____

2. eighty-two cents _____

3. two dollars and twenty cents

4. three dollars and sixty cents

_____

_____

5. 3 dimes, 2 pennies

6. 8 one-dollar bills, 4 dimes

_____

_____

7. 6 one-dollar bills, 3 pennies

8. 4 one-dollar bills, 1 dime

_____

_____

9. 6 dimes, 8 pennies

10. 5 one-dollar bills, 9 dimes

_____

_____

Find the output that equals the input.

11.

Input	Output
3 one-dollar bills	___ dimes
3 one-dollar bills	___ pennies

12.

Input	Output
6 quarters	___ dimes
6 quarters	___ pennies

Mixed Review

Add or subtract.

1. 9
   +9

2. 6
   +8

3. 3
   +9

4. 6
   +9

5. 8
   +7

6. 9
   +7

7. 13
   − 4

8. 11
   − 2

9. 12
   − 5

10. 11
    − 6

11. 13
    − 8

12. 12
    − 4

Adding Two-Digit Numbers

Add. For 1–12, check by adding up.

1.	h	t	o		2.	h	t	o		3.	h	t	o		4.	h	t	o
		5	4				6	7				4	9				3	5
+		5	4		+		5	8		+		6	1		+		7	9

5.　92
　+64

6.　30
　+73

7.　65
　+71

8.　31
　+68

9.　47
　+56

10.　39
　+88

11.　79
　+46

12.　65
　+45

13. 57 + 52 = _____　　14. 43 + 43 = _____　　15. 68 + 68 = _____

16. 47 + 59 = _____　　17. 73 + 38 = _____　　18. 87 + 35 = _____

Add mentally. Then write the answer.

19.　　2　　　　12　　　　22　　　　32　　　　42　　　　52
　　+4　　　+ 4　　　+ 4　　　+ 4　　　+ 4　　　+ 4

20.　　7　　　　17　　　　27　　　　37　　　　47　　　　57
　　+5　　　+ 5　　　+ 5　　　+ 5　　　+ 5　　　+ 5

Mixed Review

Add or subtract.

1.　4
　+5

2.　6
　+3

3.　2
　+4

4.　0
　+7

5.　3
　+5

6.　0
　+0

7.　9
　−6

8.　7
　−2

9.　6
　−4

10.　4
　−1

11.　8
　−3

12.　5
　−4

Adding Three Two-Digit Numbers

Add. Check by adding up.

1. 31
   23
   +14

2. 42
   30
   +21

3. 45
   16
   +17

4. 15
   16
   +18

5. 53
   47
   +31

6. 62
   25
   +34

7. 34
   58
   +27

8. 44
   55
   +18

9. 54
   73
   +28

10. 72
    25
    +35

11. 43
    87
    +29

12. 34
    56
    +72

13. 73 + 29 + 39 = _____

14. 47 + 28 + 16 = _____

15. 37 + 58 + 69 = _____

16. 45 + 46 + 49 = _____

17. 29 + 13 + 62 = _____

18. 19 + 27 + 82 = _____

19. 73 + 13 + 16 = _____

20. 47 + 19 + 23 = _____

Mixed Review

Compare. Write >, <, or = in each $\bigcirc$.

1. 34 $\bigcirc$ 43

2. 59 $\bigcirc$ 56

3. 71 $\bigcirc$ 71

4. 112 $\bigcirc$ 121

5. 23 − 5 $\bigcirc$ 17 + 3

6. 37 − 7 $\bigcirc$ 25 + 5

7. 12 + 31 $\bigcirc$ 25 + 22

8. 46 − 5 $\bigcirc$ 38 − 9

Use with text pages 76–77.

Problem-Solving Strategies: Find What is Extra

Cross out what is extra. Then solve the problem.

1. Ben earned $10.00. Namir earned $20.00. They each spent $5.00. How much did Ben and Namir earn together?

_____

2. Neal sold 12 apples. Mary sold 14 apples. Rick sold 8 apples. How many more apples did Neal sell than Rick?

_____

3. Carol saved $8.83. Phil saved $6.79. A puzzle costs $7.63. Can Carol buy the puzzle?

_____

4. A record album costs $6.25. A cassette tape costs $7.29. Colin has $6.75. Can he buy a tape?

_____

5. José ran 50 yards. Maria ran 30 yards. Paco ran 40 yards. How much farther did Paco run than Maria?

_____

6. Patrick jumped 4 feet in the broad jump. Mona jumped 5 feet and Teri jumped 3 feet. How much farther did Mona jump than Teri?

_____

Mixed Strategy Review

Use the picture to answer.

1. What if it is 10:30. Can Jim eat lunch in the cafeteria?

_____

CAFETERIA

OPEN FOR LUNCH
FROM 11:00 — 2:00

Solve.

2. Mrs. Bawn is pouring drinks into 15 cups for lunch. She has filled 8 of them. How many does she have left to fill?

_____

Estimating Sums

Estimate each sum.

1.   43
   +22

2.   21
   +32

3.   41
   +35

4.   42
   +71

5.   71
   +73

6.   93
   +96

7.   37
   +34

8.   81
   +56

9.   602
   +679

10.   510
   +467

11.   221
   +407

12.   218
   +340

13.   279
   +204

14.   312
   +651

15.   435
   +455

16.   704
   +805

17. 73 + 11 + 14 = _____

18. 601 + 550 = _____

19. 47 + 31 + 12 = _____

20. 627 + 316 = _____

Mixed Review

◆ Add or subtract. Use mental math or paper and pencil.

1.   3
   3
   +7

2.   4
   4
   +5

3.   7
   0
   +8

4.   9
   0
   +8

5.   5
   2
   +9

6.   2
   8
   +6

7.   17
   − 8

8.   15
   − 7

9.   15
   − 9

10.   16
   − 8

11.   18
   − 9

12.   16
   − 7

13. 14 − 6 = _____

14. 14 − 7 = _____

15. 17 − 2 = _____

Adding Three-Digit and Four-Digit Numbers

Add. For 1–16, check by adding up.

1. 522
    +747

2. 645
    +391

3. 927
    +739

4. 788
    +935

5.   28
     469
    +583

6. 595
    414
    +107

7. 667
    684
    +729

8. 145
    783
    +229

9. 6,894
    +8,796

10. 9,678
    +4,983

11. 6,825
    +5,549

12. 5,634
    +8,365

13. 9,843
    +5,045

14. 6,945
    +6,812

15. 7,648
    +8,579

16. 6,543
    +7,432

17. $7{,}983 + 6{,}748 =$ _____

18. $6{,}167 + 7{,}709 =$ _____

19. $8{,}074 + 725 =$ _____

20. $9{,}287 + 8{,}948 =$ _____

Mixed Review

Round each number to the nearest ten.

1. 37 _____   2. 41 _____   3. 65 _____   4. 78 _____

◆ Add. Use mental math or paper and pencil.

5.   45
    +42

6.   37
    +25

7.   82
    +11

8.   54
    +33

9.   49
    +32

10. 77
    +18

Name _____

Adding Money

Add.

1. $1.28
    + 4.35

2. $.69
    + .38

3. $4.96
    + 7.38

4. $16.25
    + 13.78

5. $43.39
    + 29.68

6. $68.79
    + 94.35

7. $86.15
    + 25.92

8. $39.94
    + 86.29

9. $3.52
    4.75
    + 6.63

10. $.18
    .93
    + .25

11. $48.72
    25.37
    + 16.29

12. $83.47
    62.29
    + 19.05

13. $38.42 + $74.09 = _____

14. $9.29 + $48.69 = _____

15. Julie spent $4.98 for books today and $6.72 for art supplies yesterday. How much money did she spend in all?

16. José spent $16.32 for a game last week and $8.39 for puzzles this week. How much money did he spend in all?

_____

_____

Mixed Review

◆ Add or subtract. Use mental math or paper and pencil.

1. 5
    3
    +6

2. 2
    7
    +1

3. 6
    3
    +5

4. 6
    1
    +8

5. 0
    5
    +4

6. 4
    5
    +3

7. 7
    +8

8. 4
    +4

9. 5
    +4

10. 14
    – 6

11. 17
    – 9

12. 15
    – 7

13. 16
    – 8

14. 15
    – 6

15. 16
    – 7

16. 14
    – 7

17. 16
    – 9

18. 15
    – 4

Use with text pages 100–105.

Subtracting Two-Digit Numbers

Subtract. Check by adding.

1.	tens	ones
	7	3
	−2	1

2.	tens	ones
	6	5
	−4	2

3.	tens	ones
	8	9
	−2	3

4. 40
   −20

5. 48
   −32

6. 67
   −12

7. 42
   −31

8. 46
   − 5

9. 35
   −22

10. 49
    −13

11. 53
    −20

12.	tens	ones
	6	1
	−4	9

13.	tens	ones
	5	3
	−2	9

14.	tens	ones
	3	2
	−1	6

15. 32
    −19

16. 86
    −37

17. 45
    −27

18. 50
    −18

19. $42 - 13 =$ _____   20. _____ $= 49 - 27$ 21. $63 - 15 =$ _____

Mixed Review

Add or subtract.

1. 32
   +14

2. 38
   +13

3. 25
   +11

4. 26
   +36

5. 15
   +23

6. 9
   −5

7. 7
   −2

8. 8
   −3

9. 5
   −4

10. 6
    −2

11. $19 + 23 =$ _____   12. $16 + 20 =$ _____   13. $18 + 32 =$ _____

Estimating Differences

Round to the nearest ten and estimate each difference.

1. 27 − 12	**2.** 34 − 15	**3.** 62 − 29	**4.** 65 − 55

Round to the nearest hundred and estimate each difference.

5. 354 − 217	**6.** 716 − 280	**7.** 663 − 450	**8.** 749 − 552
9. 650 − 350	**10.** 352 − 176	**11.** 322 − 101	**12.** 682 − 552

◆ Compare. Write >, <, or = in each ◯.
Choose estimation, paper and pencil, or a calculator.

13. 52 − 14 ◯ 75 − 47   **14.** 72 − 18 ◯ 42 − 13

15. 63 − 32 ◯ 68 − 21   **16.** 43 − 37 ◯ 29 − 17

17. 87 − 42 ◯ 62 − 17   **18.** 57 − 22 ◯ 63 − 24

≡≡≡ Mixed Review ≡≡≡

Give the value of the digit 6.

1. 56,125   **2.** 612,975   **3.** 41,675

_____   _____   _____

Give the value.

4.      _____

Subtracting Three-Digit Numbers

Subtract. Check by adding.

1. $\begin{array}{r} 437 \\ -222 \\ \hline \end{array}$ 2. $\begin{array}{r} 629 \\ -393 \\ \hline \end{array}$ 3. $\begin{array}{r} 315 \\ -164 \\ \hline \end{array}$ 4. $\begin{array}{r} 674 \\ -125 \\ \hline \end{array}$

5. $\begin{array}{r} 232 \\ -147 \\ \hline \end{array}$ 6. $\begin{array}{r} 423 \\ -365 \\ \hline \end{array}$ 7. $\begin{array}{r} 625 \\ -378 \\ \hline \end{array}$ 8. $\begin{array}{r} 824 \\ -635 \\ \hline \end{array}$

9. $622 - 449 =$ _____   10. $349 - 158 =$ _____

11. $767 - 352 =$ _____   12. $325 - 136 =$ _____

Complete. Find each output.

Rule: Subtract 371.

	Input	Output
13.	456	
14.	685	
15.	722	

Rule: Subtract 426.

	Input	Output
16.	857	
17.	519	
18.	613	

Mixed Review

Write each number in standard form.

1. six hundred thirty-two

2. four thousand, seven

_____   _____

Write the word name.

3. 2,715 _____

Problem-Solving Strategies: Find What Is Missing

Lucy has 16 baseball cards in her collection.
All of her cards are more than 5 years old. Of
these cards, eight are more than 10 years old.
How many of her cards are 6 years old?

1. What is the question? _____

_____

2. How many cards does Lucy have in her
collection? _____

3. How many of her cards are more than 10
years old? _____

4. How many of her cards are less than 10
years old? _____

5. What is the greatest number of cards that
could be 6 years old? _____

6. Does Lucy have some cards that are at
least 6 years old? _____

7. Do you have enough information to tell
exactly how many cards are 6 years old? _____

Mixed Strategy Review

Solve by using problem-solving strategies.

1. What is the cost of 2 pencils and

   1 eraser? _____

2. About how many crayons would fit

   around this page? _____

PRICE LIST	
Crayons	89¢
Pencil	20¢
Eraser	35¢
Paper	45¢

Subtracting Across Zeros

Subtract. Estimate to be sure your answers
make sense.

1. 600
   − 563

2. 805
   − 284

3. 400
   − 289

4. 602
   − 474

5. 704
   − 386

6. 800
   − 659

7. 402
   − 125

8. 702
   − 196

9. 405 − 88 = _____

10. 502 − 193 = _____

11. 300 − 284 = _____

12. 207 − 128 = _____

◆ Find the correct difference. Choose mental
math or paper and pencil. Circle your answer.

13. 807 − 208
   a. 599
   b. 699
   c. 601

14. 250 − 117
   a. 143
   b. 133
   c. 147

15. 600 − 256
   a. 456
   b. 353
   c. 344

16. 300 − 197
   a. 203
   b. 103
   c. 113

17. 540 − 206
   a. 236
   b. 346
   c. 334

18. 907 − 259
   a. 656
   b. 752
   c. 648

Mixed Review

Compare. Write >, <, or = in each ◯ .

1. 1,742 ◯ 1,724

2. 6,127 ◯ 6,227

3. 3,110 ◯ 3,101

4. 4,223 ◯ 4,223

Use estimation to choose the letter of the correct answer.

5. 592 + 215   a. 707   b. 383   c. 807

Subtracting Greater Numbers

Subtract. Check by adding.

1. 8,769
   − 6,548

2. 7,695
   − 5,456

3. 8,740
   − 2,270

4. 6,875
   − 5,769

5. 7,824
   − 3,089

6. 9,536
   − 6,287

7. 9,924
   − 5,447

8. 6,943
   − 2,678

9. 8,521
   − 6,339

10. 6,105
   − 1,876

11. 3,001
   − 1,246

12. 8,240
   − 2,683

13. 4,117 − 1,238 = _____

14. 7,143 − 3,864 = _____

15. 6,542 − 2,719 = _____

16. 5,945 − 4,856 = _____

17. The odometer on Mr. Brown's car reads 7,148 miles. It read 5,795 miles three months ago. How far did Mr. Johnson drive in three months?

18. The odometer on Mrs. O'Key's car reads 9,206 miles. It read 6,789 miles two months ago. How far did Mrs. O'Key drive in two months?

_____

_____

=========== **Mixed Review** ===========

Add or subtract.

1. 35
   42
   + 37

2. 68
   31
   + 25

3. 73
   64
   + 89

4. 38
   47
   + 65

5. 22
   37
   + 63

6. 91
   27
   + 36

7. 12
   − 6

8. 11
   − 3

9. 12
   − 7

10. 13
   − 9

11. 11
   − 2

12. 13
   − 5

13. 35 + 18 + 63 = _____

14. 27 + 91 + 33 = _____

15. 9 − 5 = _____

16. 13 − 3 = _____

Subtracting Money

Subtract. Check by adding.

1. $6.79
   − 2.29

2. $6.87
   − 3.41

3. $9.43
   − 6.87

4. $12.50
   − 9.99

5. $10.11
   − 9.95

6. $11.85
   − 3.74

7. $27.41
   − 13.67

8. $8.43
   − 6.50

9. $25.00
   − 16.58

10. $22.41
    − 3.57

11. $23.99
    − 14.78

12. $29.76
    − 15.89

13. $38.39 − $18.39 = _____

14. $42.03 − $25.17 = _____

15. $51.08 − $36.16 = _____

16. $46.95 − $39.62 = _____

17. $12.35 − $2.05 = _____

18. $57.16 − $11.15 = _____

19. Sandy paid $8.63 for a record. How much change did she receive from $20.00?

20. Dana paid $6.89 for a record. How much change did she receive from $10.00?

_____   _____

Mixed Review

Add.

1. 324
   + 410

2. 623
   + 135

3. 217
   + 382

4. 421
   + 437

Compare. Write >, <, or = in each ◯ .

5. 427 − 152 ◯ 317 − 112

6. 677 − 327 ◯ 546 − 236

Telling, Using, and Estimating Time

Write each time in two ways.

1.

2.

3.

_____

_____

_____

_____

_____

_____

Tell what time it will be.

4. in 3 hours

5. in 5 hours

6. in 20 minutes

_____

_____

_____

About how long does it take? Choose *a* or *b*.

7. drinking milk   **a.** 5 hours   **b.** 5 minutes

8. making a phone call   **a.** 10 minutes   **b.** 10 hours

9. taking a nap   **a.** 2 hours   **b.** 2 minutes

10. taking a walk   **a.** 20 minutes   **b.** 20 hours

Mixed Review

Add.

1. 4,786
       +2,894

2. 3,747
       +1,386

3. 4,921
       +5,382

4. 5,783
       +1,207

5. 15¢ + 25¢ = _____

6. 72¢ + 21¢ = _____

Use with text pages 148–149.

Using the Calendar

JULY						
Sun.	Mon.	Tue.	Wed.	Thu.	Fri.	Sat.
		1	2	3	4	5
6	7	8	9	10	11	12
13	14	15	16	17	18	19
20	21	22	23	24	25	26
27	28	29	30	31		

Use the calendar to answer each question.

1. On which day does the month begin? _____

2. What is the date of the third Monday? _____

3. What is the date of the fourth Wednesday? _____

4. What is the date of the first Thursday? _____

5. On what day of the week is July 6? _____

6. On what day does the month end? _____

7. What is the date of the last Friday? _____

8. What is the date of the third Saturday? _____

Mixed Review

Add or subtract.

1. 235
   +141

2. 342
   +451

3. 621
   +143

4. 340
   +127

5. 470
   −143

6. 593
   − 24

7. 429
   −170

8. 362
   −238

Use with text pages 152–153.

Problem-Solving Strategies: Making a List

1. Anne has white bread, rye bread, turkey, and cheese. How many different sandwiches can she make? Make a list to show the sandwiches.

   number of sandwiches _____

Bread	Filling

2. Jim has a white sweater, a blue sweater, red pants, and blue pants. How many different ways can he wear the sweaters and pants? Make a list to show the outfits.

   number of outfits _____

Sweater	Pants

Mixed Strategy Review

Solve by using problem-solving strategies.

1. Jill has 3 cats, 2 dogs, and 2 hamsters. How many pets does Jill own?

   _____

2. Kim invited 8 friends to her party. Each of her friends brought 2 gifts. Use a drawing to find how many gifts Kim received.

   _____

Name _____

Reading Graphs

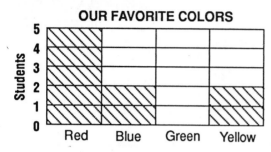

OUR FAVORITE COLORS

PETS WE HAVE

Fish	X
Dog	X X X X X
Cat	X X X
Bird	X X

Each **X** stands for 2 animals.

Use the bar graph to answer each question.

1. How many students like yellow best? _____

2. What is the most popular color? _____

3. What is the least popular color? _____

Use the pictograph to answer each question.

4. How many students own dogs? _____

5. What pet do most students have? _____

6. How many students own cats? _____

7. How many students own birds? _____

Mixed Review

Add or subtract.

1. 947 +886	2. 477 +986	3. 888 +347	4. 679 +543	5. 581 +629	6. 499 +583
7. 683 +419	8. 815 +537	9. 783 +927	10. 201 −163	11. 300 −148	12. 403 −274
13. 500 −313	14. 510 −227	15. 709 −247	16. 810 −366	17. 903 −200	18. 507 −198

Using Ordered Pairs to Locate Points

Use the grid to answer each question.

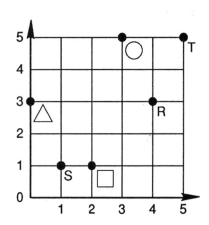

1. What ordered pair gives the location of the square?

   _____

2. What ordered pair gives the location of *R*?

   _____

3. What ordered pair gives the location of the circle?

   _____

4. What ordered pair gives the location of the triangle?

   _____

5. What ordered pair gives the location of *S*?

   _____

6. What ordered pair gives the location of *T*?

   _____

Mixed Review

Add or subtract.

1.   28
      31
    +45

2.   72
      83
    + 9

3.   16
      83
    +94

4.   321
    −198

5.   611
    −294

6.   323
    −167

7.   227
    −105

8.   643
    −271

9. 62 + 47 + 15

   _____

10. 17 + 21 + 84

   _____

Name _____

Using Patterns to Multiply

Solve.

1. 2 + 2 + 2 = _____

How many 2s? _____

_____ 2s = _____

2. 3 + 3 + 3 = _____

How many 3s? _____

_____ 3s = _____

3. 4 + 4 + 4 + 4 = _____

4 × 4 = _____

4. 5 + 5 = _____

2 × 5 = _____

5. 9 + 9 = _____

2 × 9 = _____

6. 6 + 6 + 6 = _____

3 × 6 = _____

7. 5 + 5 + 5 = _____

3 × 5 = _____

8. 7 + 7 = _____

2 × 7 = _____

9. 2 + 2 + 2 + 2 = _____

4 × 2 = _____

10. 4 + 4 + 4 = _____

3 × 4 = _____

11. 3 + 3 + 3 + 3 = _____

4 × 3 = _____

12. 7 + 7 + 7 = _____

3 × 7 = _____

Mixed Review

Tell what time it will be in 3 hours.

1. 7:00 _____

2. 10:30 _____

Write the ordered pair for each point.

3. A _____

4. B _____

5. C _____

6. D _____

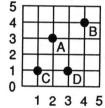

Use with text pages 172–177.

Using More Patterns to Multiply

Write a multiplication fact for each.

1.
```
*  *  *  *  *
*  *  *  *  *
```

2.
```
*  *  *
*  *  *
*  *  *
```

2 rows of 5

3 rows of 3

_____ × _____ = _____

_____ × _____ = _____

Draw a picture for each sentence. Then find each product.

3. $2 \times 9 =$ _____

4. $3 \times 4 =$ _____

$9 \times 2 =$ _____

$4 \times 3 =$ _____

5. $3 \times 2 =$ _____

6. $2 \times 4 =$ _____

$2 \times 3 =$ _____

$4 \times 2 =$ _____

Complete. Use the order property.

7. $8 \times 5 = 5 \times$ _____

8. $4 \times$ _____ $= 6 \times 4$

9. $7 \times$ _____ $= 2 \times 7$

10. $6 \times 2 = 2 \times$ _____

Mixed Review

Use the pictograph to answer the question.

1. How many beagles do the students own?

DOGS WE OWN	
Beagle	🐕 🐕 🐕
Collie	🐕 🐕
Poodle	🐕

Each 🐕 stands for 4 dogs.

_____

About how long does it take? Choose a or b.

2. eat dinner   a. 20 minutes   b. 20 hours

3. change clothes   a. 5 minutes   b. 5 hours

Use with text pages 178–181.

Using 2 and 3 as Factors

Find each product.

1.	4 ×2	2.	2 ×1	3.	6 ×2	4.	2 ×3	5.	5 ×2
6.	2 ×2	7.	7 ×2	8.	9 ×2	9.	2 ×4	10.	2 ×3
11.	3 ×3	12.	6 ×3	13.	3 ×5	14.	7 ×3	15.	3 ×8

16. $3 \times 7 =$ _____

17. $3 \times 9 =$ _____

18. $3 \times 4 =$ _____

19. $8 \times 3 =$ _____

20. $9 \times 2 =$ _____

21. $7 \times 3 =$ _____

22. $6 \times 2 =$ _____

23. $9 \times 3 =$ _____

24. $5 \times 2 =$ _____

Solve.

25. There were 7 stools. Each stool had 3 legs. How many legs were there in all?

_____

26. There are 6 boys. Each boy has 2 toy cars. How many cars are there in all?

_____

Mixed Review

Add or subtract.

1.	6 +7	2.	9 +9	3.	8 +7	4.	8 +9	5.	6 +5	6.	8 +8
7.	34 −19	8.	63 −28	9.	72 −53	10.	80 −43	11.	58 −29	12.	63 −39

Name _____

Use with text pages 182–183.

Using 0 and 1 as Factors

Find each product.

| 1. $6 \atop \times 0$ | 2. $1 \atop \times 3$ | 3. $0 \atop \times 4$ | 4. $0 \atop \times 9$ | 5. $5 \atop \times 1$ | 6. $1 \atop \times 8$ |

7. $6 \times 0 =$ _____   8. $1 \times 7 =$ _____   9. $0 \times 4 =$ _____

10. $8 \times 0 =$ _____   11. $1 \times 9 =$ _____   12. $0 \times 8 =$ _____

◆ Compare. Write $>$, $<$, or $=$ in each ◯ .
Choose mental math or paper and pencil.

13. $8 \times 1 \bigcirc 12 \times 0$ 14. $15 \times 0 \bigcirc 10 \times 0$

15. $21 \times 1 \bigcirc 12 \times 1$ 16. $469 \times 1 \bigcirc 1 \times 496$

17. $14 \times 1 \bigcirc 96 \times 0$ 18. $11 \times 1 \bigcirc 41 \times 1$

Find each missing number.

19. $3 \times 4 \times$ _____ $= 12$ 20. $2 \times$ _____ $\times 3 = 0$

21. $23 \times 1 \times$ _____ $= 23$ 22. $3 \times 6 \times$ _____ $= 18$

23. $4 \times$ _____ $\times 2 = 8$ 24. $9 \times 2 \times$ _____ $= 0$

Mixed Review

| 1. $5 \atop {2 \atop +7}$ | 2. $6 \atop {1 \atop +8}$ | 3. $3 \atop {4 \atop +0}$ | 4. $4 \atop {1 \atop +8}$ |

| 5. $983 \atop {-165}$ | 6. $841 \atop {-322}$ | 7. $629 \atop {-431}$ | 8. $739 \atop {-553}$ |

© Silver, Burdett & Ginn Inc.

Name _____

Problem-Solving Strategies: Finding Patterns

Find and complete each pattern.

1. green, blue, red, green, blue, _____

2. △, ○, □, △, ○, _____, _____, _____, _____

3. C, D, E, C, D, _____, _____, _____, _____

4. ABC, BCD, CDE, _____, _____, FGH

5. 3, 6, 9, 12, _____, _____, _____, _____

6. 10, 20, 30, 40, _____, _____, _____, _____

7. 5¢, 15¢, 25¢, 35¢, _____, _____, _____, _____

8. 110, 210, 310, _____, _____, _____, _____, _____

9. 60, _____, 50, 45, 40, _____, 30, 25

10. 1, 10, 100, _____, _____, 100,000

11. 36, 30, 24, _____, 12, _____, _____

12. $5.00, $4.50, $4.00, _____, _____, _____

Mixed Strategy Review

Draw a line through the extra information.
Then solve.

1. Todd has 3 cats and 8 fish. He also has 23 baseball cards. How many pets does Todd have?

_____

Use the drawing to solve.

2. Betsy has 9 dimes in her purse. She spent 2 of them. How many dimes does Betsy have left?

_____

38

Use with text pages 188–191.

Using 4 and 5 as Factors

Find each product.

1. $\begin{array}{r} 4 \\ \times 2 \\ \hline \end{array}$
2. $\begin{array}{r} 4 \\ \times 4 \\ \hline \end{array}$
3. $\begin{array}{r} 5 \\ \times 7 \\ \hline \end{array}$
4. $\begin{array}{r} 4 \\ \times 1 \\ \hline \end{array}$
5. $\begin{array}{r} 5 \\ \times 3 \\ \hline \end{array}$

6. $\begin{array}{r} 4 \\ \times 5 \\ \hline \end{array}$
7. $\begin{array}{r} 9 \\ \times 4 \\ \hline \end{array}$
8. $\begin{array}{r} 6 \\ \times 5 \\ \hline \end{array}$
9. $\begin{array}{r} 4 \\ \times 4 \\ \hline \end{array}$
10. $\begin{array}{r} 8 \\ \times 5 \\ \hline \end{array}$

11. $\begin{array}{r} 6 \\ \times 4 \\ \hline \end{array}$
12. $\begin{array}{r} 1 \\ \times 5 \\ \hline \end{array}$
13. $\begin{array}{r} 0 \\ \times 4 \\ \hline \end{array}$
14. $\begin{array}{r} 5 \\ \times 9 \\ \hline \end{array}$
15. $\begin{array}{r} 0 \\ \times 5 \\ \hline \end{array}$

16. $7 \times 4 =$ _____
17. $9 \times 5 =$ _____
18. $7 \times 5 =$ _____

19. $8 \times 4 =$ _____
20. $5 \times 4 =$ _____
21. $6 \times 5 =$ _____

22. $5 \times 5 =$ _____
23. $4 \times 3 =$ _____
24. $2 \times 5 =$ _____

Solve.

25. Kim has 5 pages of pictures. She has 4 pictures on each page. How many pictures does Kim have?

_____

Mixed Review

Round each number to the nearest ten.

1. 35 _____
2. 21 _____
3. 42 _____
4. 57 _____

Round each number to the nearest hundred.

5. 111 _____
6. 217 _____
7. 481 _____
8. 154 _____

Using 0 Through 5 as Factors

Find each product.

1.	2.	3.	4.	5.
3	4	3	5	4
×3	×3	×4	×2	×2

6.	7.	8.	9.	10.
4	5	2	3	4
×0	×3	×7	×6	×4

11.	12.	13.	14.	15.
4	6	1	7	3
×8	×4	×8	×5	×9

16. $1 \times 2 =$ _____   17. $3 \times 2 =$ _____   18. $1 \times 6 =$ _____

19. $5 \times 4 =$ _____   20. $3 \times 7 =$ _____   21. $8 \times 0 =$ _____

22. $4 \times 2 =$ _____   23. $5 \times 5 =$ _____   24. $0 \times 1 =$ _____

Solve.

25. Bill has 6 boxes. He has 4
rocks in each box. How many
rocks does Bill have?   _____

≡ Mixed Review ≡

Tell what time it will be in 4 hours.

1. 3:45 _____   2. 9:15 _____   3. 11:00 _____

Add.

4. $3 + 5 + 8 =$ _____   5. $2 + 6 + 7 =$ _____

6. $21 + 13 + 16 =$ _____   7. $12 + 42 + 23 =$ _____

Using 6 as a Factor

Find each product.

1. $\begin{array}{r} 6 \\ \times 3 \\ \hline \end{array}$
2. $\begin{array}{r} 4 \\ \times 6 \\ \hline \end{array}$
3. $\begin{array}{r} 2 \\ \times 6 \\ \hline \end{array}$
4. $\begin{array}{r} 6 \\ \times 5 \\ \hline \end{array}$
5. $\begin{array}{r} 6 \\ \times 1 \\ \hline \end{array}$

6. $\begin{array}{r} 6 \\ \times 7 \\ \hline \end{array}$
7. $\begin{array}{r} 5 \\ \times 6 \\ \hline \end{array}$
8. $\begin{array}{r} 9 \\ \times 6 \\ \hline \end{array}$
9. $\begin{array}{r} 6 \\ \times 8 \\ \hline \end{array}$
10. $\begin{array}{r} 0 \\ \times 6 \\ \hline \end{array}$

11. $6 \times 2 =$ _____
12. $7 \times 6 =$ _____
13. $1 \times 6 =$ _____

14. _____ $= 4 \times 6$
15. _____ $= 6 \times 6$
16. _____ $= 8 \times 6$

17. $6 \times 3 =$ _____
18. $6 \times 2 =$ _____
19. $9 \times 6 =$ _____

Solve.

20. Lyla pasted 5 pictures on each poster. She has 6 posters. How many pictures does Lyla have? _____

21. Terry has 6 plants. He put 3 drops of plant food in each pot. How many drops of plant food did he use? _____

Mixed Review

◆ Add or subtract. Use mental math or paper and pencil.

1. $\begin{array}{r} 6 \\ 2 \\ +3 \\ \hline \end{array}$
2. $\begin{array}{r} 5 \\ 1 \\ +8 \\ \hline \end{array}$
3. $\begin{array}{r} 6 \\ 0 \\ +7 \\ \hline \end{array}$
4. $\begin{array}{r} 2 \\ 4 \\ +5 \\ \hline \end{array}$
5. $\begin{array}{r} 5 \\ 4 \\ +1 \\ \hline \end{array}$
6. $\begin{array}{r} 9 \\ 0 \\ +5 \\ \hline \end{array}$

7. $\begin{array}{r} 621 \\ -189 \\ \hline \end{array}$
8. $\begin{array}{r} 333 \\ -145 \\ \hline \end{array}$
9. $\begin{array}{r} 412 \\ -143 \\ \hline \end{array}$
10. $\begin{array}{r} 622 \\ -153 \\ \hline \end{array}$
11. $\begin{array}{r} 294 \\ -187 \\ \hline \end{array}$
12. $\begin{array}{r} 721 \\ -539 \\ \hline \end{array}$

Use with text pages 206–207.

Using 7 and 8 as Factors

Find each product.

1. $\begin{array}{r} 7 \\ \times 3 \\ \hline \end{array}$
2. $\begin{array}{r} 8 \\ \times 2 \\ \hline \end{array}$
3. $\begin{array}{r} 6 \\ \times 7 \\ \hline \end{array}$
4. $\begin{array}{r} 8 \\ \times 4 \\ \hline \end{array}$
5. $\begin{array}{r} 3 \\ \times 8 \\ \hline \end{array}$

6. $\begin{array}{r} 8 \\ \times 7 \\ \hline \end{array}$
7. $\begin{array}{r} 8 \\ \times 8 \\ \hline \end{array}$
8. $\begin{array}{r} 5 \\ \times 7 \\ \hline \end{array}$
9. $\begin{array}{r} 6 \\ \times 8 \\ \hline \end{array}$
10. $\begin{array}{r} 7 \\ \times 7 \\ \hline \end{array}$

11. $8 \times 0 =$ _____
12. $7 \times 4 =$ _____
13. $5 \times 8 =$ _____

14. _____ $= 8 \times 4$
15. _____ $= 7 \times 9$
16. _____ $= 2 \times 7$

Solve.

17. Patti made 4 necklaces. She used 8 beads for each. How many beads did Patti use? _____

18. Ken rode his bike 2 miles every day. How far did he ride in 7 days? _____

Mixed Review

Add or subtract.

1. $\begin{array}{r} 1,845 \\ +3,569 \\ \hline \end{array}$
2. $\begin{array}{r} 3,769 \\ +2,483 \\ \hline \end{array}$
3. $\begin{array}{r} 2,764 \\ +4,453 \\ \hline \end{array}$
4. $\begin{array}{r} 3,107 \\ +4,200 \\ \hline \end{array}$

5. $\begin{array}{r} 5,312 \\ +2,418 \\ \hline \end{array}$
6. $\begin{array}{r} 1,810 \\ +6,204 \\ \hline \end{array}$
7. $\begin{array}{r} 600 \\ -229 \\ \hline \end{array}$
8. $\begin{array}{r} 800 \\ -347 \\ \hline \end{array}$

9. $\begin{array}{r} 203 \\ -117 \\ \hline \end{array}$
10. $\begin{array}{r} 408 \\ -169 \\ \hline \end{array}$
11. $\begin{array}{r} 300 \\ -148 \\ \hline \end{array}$
12. $\begin{array}{r} 700 \\ -613 \\ \hline \end{array}$

Using 9 as a Factor

Find each product.

1. 9
   ×3

2. 9
   ×2

3. 6
   ×9

4. 9
   ×4

5. 3
   ×9

6. 9
   ×7

7. 9
   ×8

8. 5
   ×9

9. 4
   ×9

10. 9
    ×9

11. $9 \times 0 =$ _____

12. $9 \times 4 =$ _____

13. $5 \times 9 =$ _____

14. _____ $= 3 \times 9$

15. _____ $= 9 \times 1$

16. _____ $= 9 \times 6$

Solve.

17. Chad has 9 model planes on each shelf in his room. He has 3 shelves. How many model planes does Chad have? _____

18. Karen put 4 pumpkin seeds in each hole. She had dug 9 holes. How many pumpkin seeds did she plant? _____

Mixed Review

Add or subtract.

1. 84
   +76

2. 793
   +201

3. 483
   +212

4. 86
   +29

5. 348
   +929

6. 438
   −129

7. 614
   −289

8. 98
   −47

9. $942 - 611 =$ ___

10. $764 - 531 =$ ___

11. $379 - 163 =$ ___

Problem-Solving Strategies: Using Patterns

Read and solve each problem.

1. Tony reads 1 page every 2 minutes. At 3:00, Tony began reading on page 1. When did he finish page 6? _____

2. A different TV show begins every half hour. How many TV shows are on between 6:00 and 8:00? _____

3. Pedro is sorting loose nails into bins. He fills 3 bins each afternoon. How many bins will be filled at the end of the fourth afternoon? _____

4. Julie painted this pattern on her wall. If it continues for 9 more shapes, what will the last shape be? _____

5. Mr. Taylor painted this pattern on his classroom wall. If it continues for 8 more shapes, what will the last shape be? _____

Mixed Strategy Review

Cross out the extra information. Then solve.

1. Henry had 7 cups. Ray had 4 cups. Henry filled each cup with 4 strawberries. How many strawberries did Henry have? _____

2. Lauren bought a 12-inch ruler at the store. Her total bill was 57¢. She gave the clerk 3 quarters. Her change was 6 coins. What were the coins? _____

Name _____

Using Patterns to Multiply

Multiply mentally.

1.	2.	3.	4.	5.
0 ×9	4 ×2	2 ×7	4 ×6	3 ×7

6.	7.	8.	9.	10.
1 ×1	3 ×3	5 ×2	3 ×9	4 ×5

11. $8 \times 2 =$ _____   12. $1 \times 5 =$ _____   13. $0 \times 4 =$ _____

14. $2 \times 2 =$ _____   15. $2 \times 4 =$ _____   16. $3 \times 8 =$ _____

17. $4 \times 6 =$ _____   18. $2 \times 9 =$ _____   19. $7 \times 1 =$ _____

Solve.

20. The pet store owner keeps 4 hamsters in each cage. He has 5 cages. How many hamsters are in the pet store?   _____

21. Maxwell collects seashells. He keeps them in boxes. Maxwell has 4 boxes with 7 shells in each. How many seashells does he have?   _____

22. Pencils sell for 8¢. How much will it cost to buy 4 pencils?   _____

Mixed Review

Add or subtract.

1.	2.	3.	4.	5.
5 2 +7	6 1 +8	3 4 +0	4 1 +6	6 2 +4

6. $983 - 165 =$ _____   7. $841 - 322 =$ _____   8. $739 - 553 =$ _____

Using More Patterns to Multiply

Multiply.

1. 2 × 2 = _____   2. 4 × 2 = _____   3. 5 × 2 = _____

   2 × 3 = _____   4 × 3 = _____   5 × 3 = _____

   2 × 4 = _____   4 × 4 = _____   5 × 4 = _____

   2 × 5 = _____   4 × 5 = _____   5 × 5 = _____

4. 3 × 7 = _____   5. 7 × 7 = _____   6. 9 × 7 = _____

   3 × 8 = _____   7 × 8 = _____   9 × 8 = _____

   3 × 9 = _____   7 × 9 = _____   9 × 9 = _____

7. 2 × 9 = _____   8. 4 × 3 = _____   9. 2 × 6 = _____

   9 × 2 = _____   3 × 4 = _____   6 × 2 = _____

10. 3 × 8 = _____   11. 5 × 6 = _____   12. 4 × 8 = _____

    8 × 3 = _____   6 × 5 = _____   8 × 4 = _____

13. 4 × 7 = _____   14. 5 × 8 = _____   15. 6 × 7 = _____

    7 × 4 = _____   8 × 5 = _____   7 × 6 = _____

Mixed Review

Add.

1. 5 + 5 + 5 = _____   2. 4 + 4 + 4 = _____

3. 2,375   4. 4,271   5. 6,412
   + 156   + 327   + 539

6. 4,162   7. 1,498   8. 5,055
   +3,475   +8,364   +2,407

Multiplying Three Numbers

Multiply.

1. 2 × 2 × 3 = ____

2. 3 × 2 × 1 = ____

3. 7 × 0 × 4 = ____

4. 5 × 1 × 4 = ____

5. 4 × 1 × 8 = ____

6. 3 × 4 × 1 = ____

7. 7 × 1 × 8 = ____

8. 8 × 0 × 9 = ____

9. 3 × 1 × 8 = ____

10. 2 × 3 × 1 = ____

11. 5 × 4 × 1 = ____

12. 3 × 2 × 4 = ____

13. 2 × 2 × 4 = ____

14. 2 × 3 × 2 = ____

15. 2 × 3 × 3 = ____

16. 4 × 1 × 2 = ____

17. 2 × 4 × 2 = ____

18. 5 × 1 × 3 = ____

19. 6 × 9 × 0 = ____

20. 4 × 2 × 8 = ____

Mixed Review

◆ Add or subtract. Use mental math or paper and pencil.

1.	2.	3.	4.	5.	6.
3	1	8	5	4	3
5	8	6	5	4	2
+4	+1	+1	+2	+3	+5

7.	8.	9.	10.
961	887	745	268
−479	−635	−378	−194

Using 2 and 3 as Divisors

Write a division fact for each.
Then write how many are in each group.

1. 8 animals
   4 equal groups

2. 9 birds
   3 equal groups

_____   _____

Divide.

3. $12 \div 3 = \underline{}$ 　　4. $2 \div 2 = \underline{}$ 　　5. $14 \div 2 = \underline{}$

6. $18 \div 3 = \underline{}$ 　　7. $12 \div 2 = \underline{}$ 　　8. $27 \div 3 = \underline{}$

9. $21 \div 3 = \underline{}$ 　　10. $18 \div 2 = \underline{}$ 　　11. $10 \div 2 = \underline{}$

12. $16 \div 2 = \underline{}$ 　　13. $15 \div 3 = \underline{}$ 　　14. $6 \div 3 = \underline{}$

15. $2\overline{)6}$ 　　　　16. $3\overline{)24}$ 　　　　17. $3\overline{)18}$

18. $3\overline{)27}$ 　　　　19. $3\overline{)3}$ 　　　　20. $2\overline{)4}$

Mixed Review

Add, subtract, or multiply.

1. $\begin{array}{r} 23 \\ +41 \\ \hline \end{array}$ 　　2. $\begin{array}{r} 12 \\ +23 \\ \hline \end{array}$ 　　3. $\begin{array}{r} 16 \\ +33 \\ \hline \end{array}$ 　　4. $\begin{array}{r} 45 \\ +34 \\ \hline \end{array}$

5. $\begin{array}{r} 35 \\ -12 \\ \hline \end{array}$ 　　6. $\begin{array}{r} 67 \\ -43 \\ \hline \end{array}$ 　　7. $\begin{array}{r} 89 \\ -25 \\ \hline \end{array}$ 　　8. $\begin{array}{r} 93 \\ -71 \\ \hline \end{array}$

9. $\begin{array}{r} 6 \\ \times 2 \\ \hline \end{array}$ 　　10. $\begin{array}{r} 5 \\ \times 3 \\ \hline \end{array}$ 　　11. $\begin{array}{r} 8 \\ \times 2 \\ \hline \end{array}$ 　　12. $\begin{array}{r} 9 \\ \times 3 \\ \hline \end{array}$

Using 4 and 5 as Divisors

Divide.

1. 8 ÷ 4 = ___   2. 12 ÷ 4 = ___   3. 4 ÷ 4 = ___

4. 16 ÷ 4 = ___   5. 10 ÷ 5 = ___   6. 25 ÷ 5 = ___

7. 24 ÷ 4 = ___   8. 36 ÷ 4 = ___   9. 15 ÷ 5 = ___

10. 36 ÷ 4 = ___   11. 45 ÷ 5 = ___   12. 40 ÷ 5 = ___

Complete. Follow each rule.

Rule: Divide by 5.

	Input	Output
13.	5	
14.	10	
15.	15	
16.	20	

Rule: Divide by 4.

	Input	Output
17.	4	
18.	12	
19.	16	
20.	28	

Mixed Review

Add, subtract, or multiply.

1.   27
  +17

2.   15
  +26

3.   71
  −19

4.   63
  −34

5.   7
  ×4

6.   3
  ×4

7.   9
  ×4

8.   6
  ×4

Use with text pages 244–245.

Problem-Solving Strategies: Two-Step Problems

Read each problem and solve.

1. Jean had $5.00. She spent $2.25 in one store and $1.30 in another store. How much money does she have left?

   _____

2. Frank, Sal, and Travis were in a 500 m relay race. Frank ran 150 m, Sal ran 175 m. How far did Travis run?

   _____

3. Cindy picked 3 bunches of flowers. Each bunch had 6 flowers. She gave 1 bunch of flowers to her mother. How many flowers does Cindy have left?

   _____

4. Lisa's sister babysat for the Johnsons for 3 hours. She then babysat for the Millers for 2 hours. She is paid $2 an hour for babysitting. How much money was Lisa's sister paid?

   _____

5. Marie read 21 pages in her book before lunch. She read 17 pages after lunch. Tommy read 32 pages after lunch. How many more pages did Marie read than Tommy?

   _____

Mixed Strategy Review

Solve by using problem-solving strategies.

1. Marsha read 175 pages. The book has 202 pages. How many pages does Marsha have left to read?

   _____

2. There are 124 pages in a book, 216 in another, and 439 in another. How many pages are in the 3 books in all?

   _____

Using 0 and 1 in Division

Find each quotient.

1. $5 \div 5 =$ ___

2. $0 \div 5 =$ ___

3. $9 \div 9 =$ ___

4. $6 \div 1 =$ ___

5. $8 \div 1 =$ ___

6. $2 \div 1 =$ ___

7. $0 \div 3 =$ ___

8. $0 \div 5 =$ ___

9. $0 \div 7 =$ ___

10. $6 \div 6 =$ ___

11. $0 \div 8 =$ ___

12. $5 \div 1 =$ ___

13. $4\overline{)0}$

14. $7\overline{)7}$

15. $1\overline{)3}$

16. $4\overline{)4}$

17. $9\overline{)0}$

18. $3\overline{)3}$

Solve.

19. Vanessa has 6 pictures. She pastes 6 pictures on each poster. How many posters can she make? _____

20. Mark made 4 birthday cards. He put 1 in each envelope. How many envelopes did he have? _____

Mixed Review

◆ Add, subtract, or multiply.
Use mental math or paper and pencil.

1. $\begin{array}{r} 31 \\ +82 \\ \hline \end{array}$

2. $\begin{array}{r} 71 \\ +63 \\ \hline \end{array}$

3. $\begin{array}{r} 80 \\ +94 \\ \hline \end{array}$

4. $\begin{array}{r} 36 \\ +72 \\ \hline \end{array}$

5. $\begin{array}{r} 478 \\ -312 \\ \hline \end{array}$

6. $\begin{array}{r} 894 \\ -123 \\ \hline \end{array}$

7. $\begin{array}{r} 675 \\ -461 \\ \hline \end{array}$

8. $\begin{array}{r} 549 \\ -123 \\ \hline \end{array}$

9. $\begin{array}{r} 8 \\ \times 5 \\ \hline \end{array}$

10. $\begin{array}{r} 6 \\ \times 5 \\ \hline \end{array}$

11. $\begin{array}{r} 9 \\ \times 5 \\ \hline \end{array}$

12. $\begin{array}{r} 3 \\ \times 5 \\ \hline \end{array}$

Name _____

Using 6 and 7 as Divisors

Divide.

1. 6)30　　　　2. 6)12　　　　3. 6)42　　　　4. 6)24

5. 7)63　　　　6. 7)49　　　　7. 7)28　　　　8. 7)21

9. 6)54　　　　10. 6)48　　　　11. 7)35　　　　12. 6)42

13. 6)6　　　　14. 6)18　　　　15. 7)7　　　　16. 7)42

17. 36 ÷ 6 = ___　　　18. 56 ÷ 7 = ___　　　19. 48 ÷ 6 = ___

Solve.

20. John has 42 postcards in his collection. He
pasted 6 postcards on each page. How
many pages did he need for his collection? _____

Mixed Review

◆ Add, subtract, or multiply.
Use mental math or paper and pencil.

1.　　27
　　　38
　　+46

2.　　38
　　　29
　　+ 4

3.　　72
　　　14
　　+36

4.　　423
　　　275
　　+　9

5.　　314
　　−167

6.　　547
　　−329

7.　　675
　　−354

8.　　453
　　−362

9. 7 × 0 = ___　　10. 4 × 1 = ___　　11. 8 × 1 = ___　　12. 6 × 1 = ___

Using 8 and 9 as Divisors

Find each quotient.

1. 8)32   2. 8)48   3. 9)27   4. 9)45

5. 9)81   6. 8)72   7. 9)54   8. 8)24

9. 8)0   10. 8)40   11. 9)18   12. 9)63

13. 9)9   14. 9)0   15. 8)64   16. 8)56

17. $36 \div 9 =$ __   18. $32 \div 8 =$ __   19. $45 \div$ __ $= 5$ 20. $8 \div 8 =$ __

21. $24 \div 8 =$ __   22. $27 \div 9 =$ __   23. $9 \div 9 =$ __   24. $18 \div 9 =$ __

Choose the correct number sentence.
Then solve the problem.

25. There were 48 chairs in the classroom. There were 8 equal rows of chairs. How many chairs were in each row?

a. $48 + 8 = \square$
b. $48 - 8 = \square$
c. $48 \times 8 = \square$
d. $48 \div 8 = \square$

_____

===== **Mixed Review** =====

Multiply or divide.

1. $6 \times 7 =$ _____   2. $4 \times 8 =$ _____   3. $7 \times 3 =$ _____

4. $25 \div 5 =$ _____   5. $7 \div 7 =$ _____   6. $14 \div 2 =$ _____

7. 6
   $\times 3$

8. 2
   $\times 8$

9. 9
   $\times 7$

10. 7
   $\times 8$

Relating Multiplication and Division Facts

Complete each fact family.

1. $7 \times 2 =$ _____

$2 \times 7 =$ _____

$14 \div$ _____ $= 7$

$14 \div 7 =$ _____

2. $4 \times 3 =$ _____

$3 \times 4 =$ _____

_____ $\div 4 = 3$

_____ $\div 3 = 4$

3. $5 \times 8 =$ _____

$8 \times 5 =$ _____

_____ $\div 8 = 5$

_____ $\div 5 = 8$

Give the other facts in each family.

4. $6 \times 8 = 48$

___ $\times$ ___ $=$ ___

___ $\div$ ___ $=$ ___

___ $\div$ ___ $=$ ___

5. $8 \times 3 = 24$

___ $\times$ ___ $=$ ___

___ $\div$ ___ $=$ ___

___ $\div$ ___ $=$ ___

6. $4 \times 7 = 28$

___ $\times$ ___ $=$ ___

___ $\div$ ___ $=$ ___

___ $\div$ ___ $=$ ___

Find the missing number.

7. $7 \times$ _____ $= 0$

8. $45 \div$ _____ $= 5$

9. _____ $\times 4 = 24$

10. $8 \times$ _____ $= 8$

11. $9 \div$ _____ $= 9$

12. $8 \times$ _____ $= 16$

13. $5 \times$ _____ $= 25$

14. $24 \div$ _____ $= 6$

15. _____ $\times 3 = 15$

16. $3 \times$ _____ $= 6$

17. _____ $\div 2 = 9$

18. $4 \times$ _____ $= 12$

Mixed Review

Add or subtract.

1. $\begin{array}{r} 87 \\ +53 \\ \hline \end{array}$

2. $\begin{array}{r} 97 \\ +66 \\ \hline \end{array}$

3. $\begin{array}{r} 67 \\ +54 \\ \hline \end{array}$

4. $\begin{array}{r} 87 \\ +49 \\ \hline \end{array}$

5. $\begin{array}{r} 317 \\ -125 \\ \hline \end{array}$

6. $\begin{array}{r} 252 \\ -161 \\ \hline \end{array}$

7. $\begin{array}{r} 348 \\ -119 \\ \hline \end{array}$

8. $\begin{array}{r} 246 \\ -158 \\ \hline \end{array}$

Reviewing Division Facts

Divide.

1. $2\overline{)12}$ 2. $2\overline{)18}$ 3. $3\overline{)24}$ 4. $3\overline{)21}$ 5. $4\overline{)20}$ 6. $4\overline{)32}$

7. $5\overline{)35}$ 8. $5\overline{)45}$ 9. $6\overline{)0}$ 10. $7\overline{)0}$ 11. $1\overline{)7}$ 12. $1\overline{)3}$

13. $6\overline{)24}$ 14. $6\overline{)54}$ 15. $6\overline{)18}$ 16. $7\overline{)49}$ 17. $7\overline{)42}$ 18. $7\overline{)63}$

19. $8\overline{)32}$ 20. $8\overline{)72}$ 21. $8\overline{)64}$ 22. $9\overline{)54}$ 23. $9\overline{)45}$ 24. $9\overline{)63}$

Complete each fact family.

25. $7 \times 5 = 35$ 26. $8 \times 6 = 48$ 27. $9 \times 8 = 72$

___ $\times$ ___ $=$ ___   ___ $\times$ ___ $=$ ___   ___ $\times$ ___ $=$ ___

___ $\div$ ___ $=$ ___   ___ $\div$ ___ $=$ ___   ___ $\div$ ___ $=$ ___

___ $\div$ ___ $=$ ___   ___ $\div$ ___ $=$ ___   ___ $\div$ ___ $=$ ___

28. $6 \times 4 = 24$ 29. $6 \times 7 = 42$ 30. $8 \times 5 = 40$

___ $\times$ ___ $=$ ___   ___ $\times$ ___ $=$ ___   ___ $\times$ ___ $=$ ___

___ $\div$ ___ $=$ ___   ___ $\div$ ___ $=$ ___   ___ $\div$ ___ $=$ ___

___ $\div$ ___ $=$ ___   ___ $\div$ ___ $=$ ___   ___ $\div$ ___ $=$ ___

Mixed Review

Add or subtract.

1. $\begin{array}{r} 341 \\ +232 \\ \hline \end{array}$ 2. $\begin{array}{r} 172 \\ +413 \\ \hline \end{array}$ 3. $\begin{array}{r} 300 \\ +161 \\ \hline \end{array}$ 4. $\begin{array}{r} 401 \\ +183 \\ \hline \end{array}$

5. $\begin{array}{r} 310 \\ -140 \\ \hline \end{array}$ 6. $\begin{array}{r} 701 \\ -451 \\ \hline \end{array}$ 7. $\begin{array}{r} 600 \\ -361 \\ \hline \end{array}$ 8. $\begin{array}{r} 810 \\ -643 \\ \hline \end{array}$

Finding and Writing Fractions

Write the fraction for the part that is shaded.

1.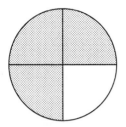

2.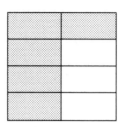

3.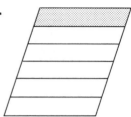

_____   _____   _____

4.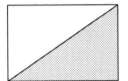

5.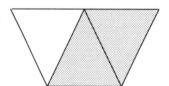

6.

_____   _____   _____

7.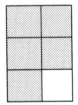

8.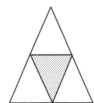

9.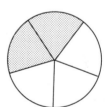

_____   _____   _____

Mixed Review

Multiply or divide.

1. $7 \times 6 =$ _____   **2.** $4 \times 8 =$ _____   **3.** $3 \times 6 =$ _____

4. $9 \times 7 =$ _____   **5.** $5 \times 6 =$ _____   **6.** $6 \times 6 =$ _____

7. $12 \div 4 =$ _____   **8.** $36 \div 9 =$ _____   **9.** $45 \div 5 =$ _____

Writing Fractions for Parts of Groups

Write a fraction for the part that is shaded.

1.

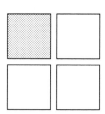

___

2.

___

3.

___

4.

___

5.

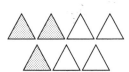

___

6.

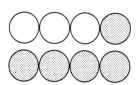

___

Mixed Review

◆ Add, subtract, multiply, or divide. Use mental math or paper and pencil.

1. 67	2. 86	3. 600	4. 101
+78	+87	−123	− 54

5. 6	6. 9	7. 4	8. 7
×9	×2	×5	×8

9. $5\overline{)45}$ **10.** $6\overline{)24}$ **11.** $8\overline{)48}$ **12.** $5\overline{)35}$

Finding Fractional Parts

Complete.

1. $\frac{1}{2}$ of 6 = ___

2. $\frac{1}{3}$ of 9 = ___

3. $\frac{1}{2}$ of 2 = ___

4. $\frac{1}{8}$ of 64 = ___

5. $\frac{1}{5}$ of 10 = ___

6. $\frac{1}{9}$ of 81 = ___

7. $\frac{1}{7}$ of 21 = ___

8. $\frac{1}{4}$ of 24 = ___

9. $\frac{1}{6}$ of 18 = ___

10. $\frac{1}{8}$ of 56 = ___

11. $\frac{1}{2}$ of 14 = ___

12. $\frac{1}{3}$ of 24 = ___

13. $\frac{1}{6}$ of 30 = ___

14. $\frac{1}{5}$ of 25 = ___

15. $\frac{1}{7}$ of 49 = ___

16. $\frac{1}{4}$ of 32 = ___

17. $\frac{1}{2}$ of 18 = ___

18. $\frac{1}{6}$ of 6 = ___

Solve.

19. There are 72 students in the band and $\frac{1}{9}$ of them are third-graders. How many students are third-graders?

_____

20. Fourth-graders make up $\frac{1}{8}$ of the band. How many students are fourth-graders?

_____

Mixed Review

Multiply or divide.

1. $\begin{array}{r} 7 \\ \times 3 \\ \hline \end{array}$

2. $\begin{array}{r} 8 \\ \times 5 \\ \hline \end{array}$

3. $\begin{array}{r} 6 \\ \times 0 \\ \hline \end{array}$

4. $\begin{array}{r} 5 \\ \times 3 \\ \hline \end{array}$

5. $\begin{array}{r} 1 \\ \times 8 \\ \hline \end{array}$

6. $7\overline{)49}$

7. $8\overline{)24}$

8. $4\overline{)16}$

9. $8\overline{)40}$

10. $9\overline{)63}$

Naming Equivalent Fractions

Use what you know about equivalent fractions
to find each missing number.

1.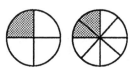

$$\frac{1}{4} = \frac{\square}{8}$$

2.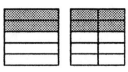

$$\frac{2}{5} = \frac{4}{\square\square}$$

3.

$$\frac{2}{3} = \frac{\square}{\square}$$

4.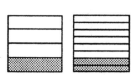

$$\frac{1}{2} = \frac{\square}{4}$$

5.

$$\frac{3}{4} = \frac{\square}{8}$$

6.

$$\frac{1}{3} = \frac{\square}{6}$$

7.

$$\frac{1}{4} = \frac{\square}{\square}$$

8.

$$\frac{4}{4} = \frac{\square}{\square}$$

9.

$$\frac{3}{3} = \frac{\square}{\square}$$

Circle the letter of the greater amount.

10.

a. $\frac{1}{4}$ of the muffins

b. $\frac{1}{3}$ of the muffins

Mixed Review

Multiply or divide.

1.
$$\begin{array}{r} 8 \\ \times 9 \\ \hline \end{array}$$

2.
$$\begin{array}{r} 9 \\ \times 7 \\ \hline \end{array}$$

3.
$$\begin{array}{r} 6 \\ \times 4 \\ \hline \end{array}$$

4.
$$\begin{array}{r} 6 \\ \times 2 \\ \hline \end{array}$$

5. $5\overline{)35}$

6. $8\overline{)24}$

Comparing Fractions

Compare. Write $>$, $<$, or $=$ in each ◯.
Use fraction pieces if you like.

1.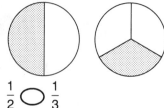

$\frac{1}{2}$ ◯ $\frac{1}{3}$

2.

$\frac{3}{4}$ ◯ $\frac{1}{2}$

3.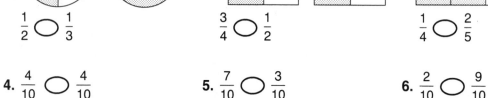

$\frac{1}{4}$ ◯ $\frac{2}{5}$

4. $\frac{4}{10}$ ◯ $\frac{4}{10}$

5. $\frac{7}{10}$ ◯ $\frac{3}{10}$

6. $\frac{2}{10}$ ◯ $\frac{9}{10}$

7. $\frac{2}{8}$ ◯ $\frac{5}{8}$

8. $\frac{1}{6}$ ◯ $\frac{1}{3}$

9. $\frac{4}{8}$ ◯ $\frac{1}{2}$

10. $\frac{1}{5}$ ◯ $\frac{1}{6}$

11. $\frac{3}{5}$ ◯ $\frac{3}{4}$

12. $\frac{6}{8}$ ◯ $\frac{3}{4}$

13. $\frac{4}{10}$ ◯ $\frac{2}{5}$

14. $\frac{5}{8}$ ◯ $\frac{7}{8}$

15. $\frac{3}{6}$ ◯ $\frac{1}{3}$

16. $\frac{1}{5}$ ◯ $\frac{3}{4}$

17. $\frac{3}{4}$ ◯ $\frac{1}{4}$

18. $\frac{3}{10}$ ◯ $\frac{9}{10}$

Solve.

19. Jan used $\frac{1}{3}$ of a can of paint.
Terry used $\frac{3}{8}$ of a can. Who
used more paint?

_____

20. Diane's glass of juice is $\frac{2}{3}$ full.
Peter's glass is $\frac{1}{2}$ full. Whose
glass has more juice in it?

_____

Mixed Review

Multiply or divide.

1. $\begin{array}{r} 4 \\ \times 5 \\ \hline \end{array}$

2. $\begin{array}{r} 6 \\ \times 8 \\ \hline \end{array}$

3. $7\overline{)28}$

4. $5\overline{)35}$

5. $6\overline{)36}$

Naming Mixed Numbers

Write the mixed number for the part that is shaded.

1.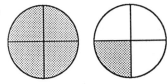

2.

————

3.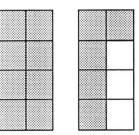

4.

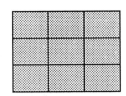

————

————

Use the picture to solve.

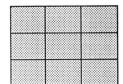 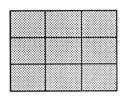 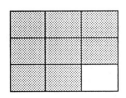

5. Write a mixed number for the shaded part.

6. Write a fraction for the unshaded part.

————

————

Problem-Solving Strategies: Making and Using Tables

Complete the table. Answer the questions.

VOLUNTEER HOSPITAL HELP SCHEDULE			
Assistant	Number of Days Worked per Week	Number of Hours Worked per Day	Total Hours Worked per Week
Mindy	2	4	8
1. Frank	4		12
2. Ramone		5	20
3. Leslie	3	5	
4. Carmen	3	3	

5. Who worked the greatest number of hours per week?

_____

6. Who worked the least number of hours per week?

_____

7. Who worked the least number of days per week?

_____

8. How many hours did Mindy and Frank work per week?

_____

9. Who worked the greatest number of days per week?

_____

10. What was the total number of hours worked that week?

_____

Mixed Strategy Review

Cross out the extra information. Then solve.

Tia jumped rope 120 times.
Clara jumped 172 times.
Sandra jumped 134 times.
How many more times did Sandra
jump rope than Tia?

_____

Exploring Probability

Circle the letter of the correct answer.

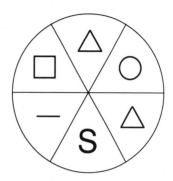

1. The chance of the pointer stopping on □ is?

    a. 1 out of 4

    b. 1 out of 6

    c. 1 out of 3

2. The chance of the pointer stopping on **S** is?

    a. 1 out of 4

    b. 1 out of 6

    c. 2 out of 6

3. The chance of the pointer stopping on △ is?

    a. 1 out of 4

    b. 1 out of 6

    c. 2 out of 6

Use the table to answer each question.

Heads	Tails
ⵌ I	ⵌ III

4. How many times did heads show?

_____

5. How many times did tails show?

_____

6. Why are these results about the same?

_____

Mixed Review

Write the fraction or mixed number for each.

1.

2.

3.

   _____   _____   _____

Use with text pages 300–303.

Estimating and Measuring Length in Metric Units

Estimate each length. Then measure to the nearest centimeter.

1.

2.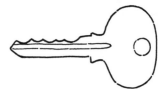

Estimate ___ cm

Measure ___ cm

Estimate ___ cm

Measure ___ cm

Choose *cm, m,* or *km* to complete each sentence.

3. The distance from St. Louis to Chicago

is about 540 _____ .

4. A pencil is about 14 _____ long.

5. The distance from home to school is

about 3 _____ .

6. The length of the school cafeteria is

about 17 _____ .

Complete.

7. 1,000 m = _____ km

8. 1 m = _____ cm

9. 100 cm _____ m

10. 2 km = _____ m

Mixed Review

Add, subtract, multiply, or divide.

1. 75 + 67 = ____

2. 62 − 34 = ____

3. 7 × 8 = ____

4. 9 × 3 = ____

5. 28 ÷ 4 = ____

6. 64 ÷ 8 = ____

Estimating Capacity with Metric Units

Choose *milliliter* or *liter* to measure each.

1. tank of oil _____

2. pitcher of milk _____

3. pot of water _____

4. teaspoon of gravy _____

5. glass of juice _____

6. raindrop _____

Choose the best estimate for each.

7. a glass of milk
   a. 150 L   b. 150 mL
   c. 500 mL   d. 5 mL

8. a bowl of soup
   a. 300 mL   b. 30 mL
   c. 300 L   d. 3 L

9. a teaspoon of water
   a. 70 L   c. 7 L
   b. 70 mL   d. 7 mL

10. a bucket of water
   a. 40 L   b. 4 L
   c. 40 mL   d. 4 mL

Compare. Write >, <, or = in each ◯ .

11. 3 L ◯ 3,000 mL

12. 4,000 mL ◯ 4,000 L

13. 1 L ◯ 7,000 mL

14. 10 L ◯ 6,999 mL

Solve.

15. Felicia has 3 L of homemade soup. Should she put it in a large pot or a small bowl? _____

Mixed Review

Add, subtract, multiply, or divide.

1. $\begin{array}{r} 61 \\ +75 \\ \hline \end{array}$

2. $\begin{array}{r} 83 \\ +42 \\ \hline \end{array}$

3. $\begin{array}{r} 75 \\ +74 \\ \hline \end{array}$

4. $\begin{array}{r} 679 \\ -123 \\ \hline \end{array}$

5. $\begin{array}{r} 578 \\ -232 \\ \hline \end{array}$

6. $\begin{array}{r} 845 \\ -721 \\ \hline \end{array}$

7. $\begin{array}{r} 6 \\ \times 4 \\ \hline \end{array}$

8. $\begin{array}{r} 8 \\ \times 4 \\ \hline \end{array}$

9. $9 \times 4 =$ ___

10. $3 \times 4 =$ ___

11. $4\overline{)20}$

12. $4\overline{)28}$

Estimating Weight with Metric Units

Choose *gram* or *kilogram* to measure each.

1. a bag of grain _____   2. a marble _____

3. a feather _____   4. a watermelon _____

5. a watch _____   6. a leaf _____

Choose the better estimate for each.

7. a dog
   a. 25 kg   b. 25 g

8. an ant
   a. 2 g   b. 2 kg

9. a zebra
   a. 200 g   b. 200 kg

10. a Ping-Pong ball
   a. 4 g   b. 4 kg

Compare. Write $>$, $<$, or $=$ in each ◯ .

11. 2 g ◯ 2 kg   12. 8 g ◯ 1 kg   13. 2,000 g ◯ 2 kg

14. 3,000 kg ◯ 1 kg   15. 5 g ◯ 5 kg   16. 1,000 g ◯ 1 kg

17. 10 g ◯ 2 g   18. 100 kg ◯ 100 kg   19. 3 kg ◯ 300 g

Solve.

20. Kiernan needs flour to bake muffins.
    Should she buy 1 kg or 1 g of flour?   _____

Mixed Review

Multiply or divide.

1. 8
   $\times 4$

2. 6
   $\times 6$

3. 7
   $\times 2$

4. 9
   $\times 3$

5. $4\overline{)8}$

6. $3\overline{)12}$

7. $3\overline{)24}$

8. $3\overline{)18}$

Problem-Solving Strategies: Alternate Solutions

◆ Solve. Use a calculator or paper and pencil.

1. Mrs. Brown has 4 children. They all need warm socks for camping. Including tax, a pair of socks costs $3. How much will Mrs. Brown spend if she buys 2 pairs of socks for each child?

   _____

2. The Rodgers family is taking a raft trip on the Meramec River. They take a 10 minute rest after each 20 minutes of paddling. They are on the raft trip for 3 hours. How much time did they spend paddling?

   _____

3. The Adventure Club is camping for the night. They put up their tents 10 ft apart in a line. There are 8 tents. How far apart are the first and last tents?

   _____

4. The members of the Adventure Club will hike to their next camping spot. They average 3 miles per hour. If they start at 7 A.M. and hike till 12 P.M., how far will they have hiked?

   _____

Mixed Strategy Review

Use the price list to solve each.

1. How much would Tim spend for a pen

   and an eraser? _____

PRICE LIST	
Notebook	69¢
Pencil	15¢
Eraser	10¢
Pen	60¢
Tax included	

2. Joyce has 25¢. How much change will

   she get if she buys a pencil? _____

3. Gary has 90¢. Can he buy a notebook

   and an eraser? _____

Estimating and Measuring Length with Customary Units

Estimate the length of each bar. Then
measure to the nearest $\frac{1}{2}$ inch.

1.

_____

2.

_____

Choose *in., ft, yd,* or *mi* to measure each.

3. length of a hallway

_____

4. distance from San Diego to Boston

_____

5. width of the classroom

_____

6. width of a notebook

_____

Complete.

7. 1 ft = _____ in.   8. 36 in. = _____ yd

9. 3 yd = _____ ft   10. 24 in. = _____ ft

Mixed Review

Write a fraction for each shaded part.

1.

_____

2.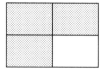

_____

3.

_____

Multiply or divide.

4. 8 × 8 = _____   5. 5 × 4 = _____   6. 7 × 2 = _____

7. 72 ÷ 9 = _____   8. 25 ÷ 5 = _____   9. 16 ÷ 4 = _____

Name _____

Estimating Capacity in Customary Units

Choose *cup, pint, quart,* or *gallon* to measure
each amount.

1. bathtub full of water _____

2. orange juice for 2 people _____

3. glass of milk _____

4. fish tank of water _____

5. pitcher of milk _____

6. hot cocoa for 1 person _____

Choose the better estimate for each.

7. a bucket of water
   a. 3 gallons   b. 3 pints

8. a tank full of gasoline
   a. 4 gallons   b. 14 gallons

9. yogurt for lunch
   a. 1 quart   b. 1 cup

10. soup for 4 people
    a. 2 pints   b. 2 gallons

Complete.

11. 2 cups = __ pint

12. 1 pint = __ cups

13. 2 pints = __ quart

14. 1 quart = __ pints

15. 2 quarts = __ pints

16. 1 gallon = __ quarts

17. 4 cups = __ pints

18. 2 gallons = __ quarts

19. 4 pints = __ cups

20. 1 gallon = __ pints

Mixed Review

Add, subtract, or multiply.

1. $3 + 3$
2. $4 + 5$
3. $3 + 6$
4. $6 - 4$
5. $4 - 4$
6. $5 - 3$

7. 2×3
8. 2×2
9. 3×3
10. 1×6
11. 4×0
12. 5×1

13. $4 \times 3 = $ _____

14. $2 \times 5 = $ _____

15. $7 \times 2 = $ _____

Use with text pages 324–329.

Estimating Weight and Reading a Fahrenheit Thermometer

Choose *ounce* or *pound* to measure each.

1. a dog _____

2. a pencil _____

3. a paper airplane _____

4. a bear _____

5. an eraser _____

6. a dictionary _____

Choose the better estimate for each.

7. a car
   a. 3,000 pounds   **b.** 30 pounds

8. a dozen eggs
   a. 2 ounces   **b.** 24 ounces

9. one apple
   a. 5 ounces   **b.** 5 pounds

10. a bag of apples
   a. 5 ounces   **b.** 5 pounds

Write each Fahrenheit temperature shown.

11.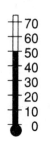

12.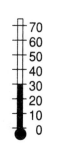

13.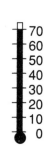

14.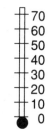

_____   _____   _____   _____

Mixed Review

Multiply or divide.

1. $7 \times 7 =$ _____

2. $6 \times 5 =$ _____

3. $4 \times 7 =$ _____

4. $35 \div 5 =$ _____

5. $24 \div 6 =$ _____

6. $16 \div 4 =$ _____

7. $7 \times 9 =$ _____

8. $4 \times 3 =$ _____

9. $6 \times 6 =$ _____

10. $45 \div 5 =$ _____

11. $21 \div 7 =$ _____

12. $18 \div 3 =$ _____

Use with text pages 338–339.

Naming Space Figures

Name each space figure.

1.

_____

2.

_____

3.

_____

4.

_____

5.

_____

6.

_____

Name the part marked by the arrow.

7.

_____

8.

_____

9.

_____

Mixed Review

◆ Add, subtract, multiply, or divide.
Use mental math or paper and pencil.

1. 12
   $+46$

2. 32
   $+42$

3. 63
   $+14$

4. 98
   -23

5. 67
   -32

6. 45
   -22

7. 9
   $\times 2$

8. 6
   $\times 6$

9. $24 \div 8 =$ _____

10. $35 \div 7 =$ _____

11. $48 \div 8 =$ _____

12. $81 \div 9 =$ _____

13. $63 \div 9 =$ _____

14. $32 \div 4 =$ _____

Name Plane Figures

Name each plane figure.

1.   2.   3.   4.

_____   _____   _____   _____

5. Which figure has no straight sides and
   no corners?   _____

6. Which figure has 3 sides and 3 corners?   _____

7. Which figure has 4 equal sides?   _____

8. Which figure has 2 pairs of equal sides?   _____

Name the first figure. Circle the letters of the same kind of figure.

9.   a.   b.   c.   d.

_____

10.   a.   b.   c.   d.

_____

Mixed Review

Add or subtract.

1. 234
   +165

2. 420
   +389

3. 754
   +208

4. 733
   +198

5. 641
   −339

6. 800
   −528

7. 529
   −311

8. 402
   −230

Use with text pages 344–347.

Naming Lines, Line Segments, Rays, and Right Angles

Name each figure.

1.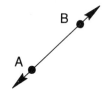

2.

3.

4.

_____ _____ _____ _____

Name the line segments in each figure.

5.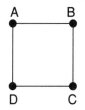

6.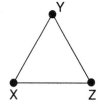

7.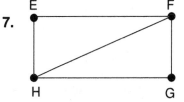

_____ _____ _____

Name the first figure. Circle the letters of the same kind of figure.

8.    **a.**   **b.**   **c.**   **d.**

_____

9.   **a.**   **b.**   **c.**   **d.**

_____

Mixed Review

Add or subtract.

1. $\begin{array}{r} 27 \\ +16 \\ \hline \end{array}$ **2.** $\begin{array}{r} 35 \\ +36 \\ \hline \end{array}$ **3.** $\begin{array}{r} 49 \\ +28 \\ \hline \end{array}$ **4.** $\begin{array}{r} 84 \\ -18 \\ \hline \end{array}$ **5.** $\begin{array}{r} 62 \\ -39 \\ \hline \end{array}$

Use with text pages 350–351.

Problem-Solving Strategies: Guess and Test

Use a guess-and-test strategy to solve these problems.

1. Juanita made 12 rows of circles and squares. She has 2 more rows of circles than of squares. How many rows of circles does she have?

_____

2. Joe has 21 squares and circles. He has 5 more squares than circles. How many squares does he have?

_____

3. There are 14 people who wish to sit at tables. Round tables seat 5 people. Square tables seat 4. How many of each table do the people need?

_____

4. What if 28 people arrive later and also wish to sit at tables. How many of each table do the newcomers need?

_____

5. Lynn has $1.65 in dimes and quarters. He has 1 more quarter than he has dimes. How many dimes does Lynn have?

_____

6. Becky has 7 coins. She has 1 quarter, and twice as many dimes as pennies. How much money does Becky have?

_____

Mixed Strategy Review

Find the pattern. Fill in the missing numbers.

1. 1, 3, 2, 4, 3, 5, 4, 6, ___, ___, ___

Solve.

2. Todd has 1 quarter, 1 nickel, and 2 dimes. Does he have enough money to buy a notebook for 39¢?

_____

3. Breakfast for 25 campers is pancakes. If each camper wants 3 pancakes, how many pancakes do they need?

_____

Use with text pages 352–355.

Naming Congruent and Symmetric Figures

Are the figures in each pair congruent?
Write *yes* or *no.*

1.

2.

3.

4.

_____   _____   _____   _____

Find the figures in each row that are congruent
to the first figure in the row.

5.   **a.**   **b.**   **c.**   **d.**

6.   **a.**   **b.**   **c.**   **d.**

Is the dashed line a line of symmetry?
Write *yes* or *no.*

7.

8.

9.

10.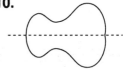

_____   _____   _____   _____

═══════ Mixed Review ═══════

Add, subtract, multiply, or divide.

1. 923
  − 378

2. 678
  + 244

3. 2,605
  − 1,206

4. 5,239
  + 4,181

5. $3 \times 6 =$ ___ **6.** $9 \times 3 =$ ___ **7.** $36 \div 6 =$ ___ **8.** $28 \div 7 =$ ___

Finding Perimeter, Area, and Volume

Find the perimeter of each figure.

1.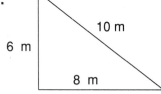

2.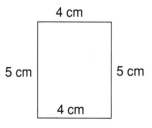

3.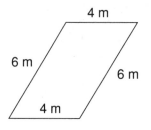

_____   _____   _____

Find the area of each figure.

4.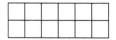

5.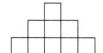

6.

_____   _____   _____

Find the volume of each figure.

7.

8.

9.

_____   _____   _____

Mixed Review

Add, subtract, multiply, or divide.

1. $\begin{array}{r} 89 \\ +76 \end{array}$

2. $\begin{array}{r} 47 \\ +83 \end{array}$

3. $\begin{array}{r} 66 \\ +74 \end{array}$

4. $\begin{array}{r} 329 \\ -144 \end{array}$

5. $\begin{array}{r} 682 \\ -234 \end{array}$

6. $\begin{array}{r} 417 \\ -132 \end{array}$

7. $\begin{array}{r} 7 \\ \times 4 \end{array}$

8. $\begin{array}{r} 3 \\ \times 4 \end{array}$

9. $8\overline{)16}$

10. $4\overline{)24}$

11. $8\overline{)40}$

12. $5\overline{)35}$

Use with text pages 370–377.

Reading and Writing Tenths and Hundredths

Write a fraction and a decimal for the shaded part.

1.

2.

3.

_____ = _____   _____ = _____   _____ = _____

Shade each figure for the fraction or the decimal.

4. $\frac{9}{10}$

5. $\frac{1}{10}$

6. 0.21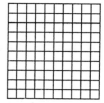

Choose the correct fraction or decimal.

7. $\frac{7}{100}$

   a. 0.01   **b.** 0.7

   c. 0.07   **d.** 0.1

8. $\frac{3}{10}$

   a. 0.03   **b.** 0.3

   c. 0.1   **d.** 3.0

9. $\frac{8}{100}$

   a. 0.8   **b.** 8.0

   c. 1.8   **d.** 0.08

Write each as a decimal.

10. sixty-one hundredths

11. 9 out of 100

12. five tenths

_____   _____   _____

Mixed Review

Multiply or divide.

1. $1 \times 6 =$ __   **2.** $3 \times 7 =$ __   **3.** $0 \times 0 =$ __   **4.** $9 \times 0 =$ __

5. $8\overline{)8}$ **6.** $3\overline{)0}$ **7.** $5\overline{)30}$ **8.** $6\overline{)18}$

Use with text pages 378–379.

Writing Decimals in Order

Choose the greater number. Circle your answer.

1. 0.25 or 0.52   2. 0.81 or 0.78   3. 0.47 or 0.27

4. 0.12 or 0.02   5. 0.09 or 0.08   6. 0.34 or 0.43

Choose two of the numbers 2, 5, or 7 to write a decimal:

7. less than 0.33. _____   8. less than 0.75. _____

9. greater than 0.5. _____   10. greater than 0.6. _____

Compare. Write >, <, or = in each ◯.

11. 0.03 ◯ 0.30   12. 0.12 ◯ 0.10   13. 0.67 ◯ 0.67

14. 0.46 ◯ 0.45   15. 0.32 ◯ 0.09   16. 0.27 ◯ 0.72

17. 0.2 ◯ 0.20   18. 0.91 ◯ 0.92   19. 0.32 ◯ 0.82

20. thirty hundredths ◯ three tenths

Mixed Review

◆ Add, subtract, multiply, or divide.
Use mental math or paper and pencil.

1. $\begin{array}{r} 0 \\ +2 \\ \hline \end{array}$ 2. $\begin{array}{r} 23 \\ -\ 0 \\ \hline \end{array}$ 3. $\begin{array}{r} 173 \\ +569 \\ \hline \end{array}$ 4. $\begin{array}{r} 432 \\ -308 \\ \hline \end{array}$ 5. $\begin{array}{r} 486 \\ -\ 80 \\ \hline \end{array}$

6. $\begin{array}{r} 9,753 \\ -5,602 \\ \hline \end{array}$ 7. $\begin{array}{r} 8,329 \\ -5,328 \\ \hline \end{array}$ 8. $\begin{array}{r} 173 \\ +569 \\ \hline \end{array}$ 9. $\begin{array}{r} 9 \\ \times 4 \\ \hline \end{array}$ 10. $\begin{array}{r} 7 \\ \times 8 \\ \hline \end{array}$

11. $\begin{array}{r} 32 \\ -27 \\ \hline \end{array}$ 12. $3\overline{)27}$ 13. $\begin{array}{r} 401 \\ +516 \\ \hline \end{array}$ 14. $\begin{array}{r} 6 \\ \times 7 \\ \hline \end{array}$ 15. $8\overline{)48}$

Name _____

Reading and Writing Decimals Greater than 1

Write a decimal for the shaded part.

1. 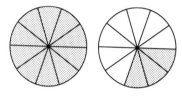 **2.**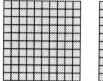

_____   _____

Write each as decimal.

3. $3\frac{2}{100}$ _____   **4.** $7\frac{9}{10}$ _____   **5.** $4\frac{4}{10}$ _____

6. nine and twenty-seven hundredths _____

7. four and five hundredths _____

8. eight and six tenths _____

9. three and twelve hundredths _____

Write in words. Name the value of the digit 3.

10. 7.13 _____

11. 4.39 _____

Choose the greater number. Circle your answer.

12. 9.4 or 9.42   **13.** 4.29 or 4.30   **14.** 5.27 or 5.17

Mixed Review

◆ Add or subtract.
Use mental math or paper and pencil.

1.	**2.**	**3.**	**4.**	**5.**
39	83	$.18	69	88
76	59	.09	7	− 79
+ 2	+ 4	+ .35	+80	

Problem-Solving Strategies: Making and Using Drawings

For each problem, make a drawing to show the facts. Use your drawing to solve the problem.

1. A frog jumps 200 cm in 1 jump. How far does it travel in 6 jumps?

_____

2. Rick walked around a square garden. Each side of the garden is 15 meters long. How far did Rick walk?

_____

3. Abe put a seashell in every window of his house. His house has 2 windows on each side downstairs. It has 3 windows on each side upstairs. How many shells did he use?

_____

Mixed Strategy Review

Solve by using problem-solving strategies.

1. Mr. Jones wants to put a fence around his garden. The garden measures 24 feet on each of 2 sides and 15 feet on each of the remaining 2 sides. How much fencing does Mr. Jones need?

_____

Complete each pattern.

2. 1, 3, 5, 2, 4, 6, 7, 9, 11, 8, 10, 12,

___, ___, ___, ___, ___, ___

3. 1, 4, 9, 16, 25, ___, ___, ___

Adding with Decimals

Add.

1. $\begin{array}{r}0.1\\+0.5\\\hline\end{array}$	**2.** $\begin{array}{r}2.7\\+0.4\\\hline\end{array}$	**3.** $\begin{array}{r}0.5\\+4.9\\\hline\end{array}$	**4.** $\begin{array}{r}0.3\\+0.8\\\hline\end{array}$
5. $\begin{array}{r}3.2\\+4.9\\\hline\end{array}$	**6.** $\begin{array}{r}1.5\\+2.5\\\hline\end{array}$	**7.** $\begin{array}{r}6.2\\+4.8\\\hline\end{array}$	**8.** $\begin{array}{r}4.1\\+6.8\\\hline\end{array}$
9. $\begin{array}{r}2.7\\+6.8\\\hline\end{array}$	**10.** $\begin{array}{r}2.5\\+5.8\\\hline\end{array}$	**11.** $\begin{array}{r}7.3\\+1.7\\\hline\end{array}$	**12.** $\begin{array}{r}5.8\\+2.9\\\hline\end{array}$

13. $1.1 + 2.2 =$ _____ **14.** $2.4 + 5.1 =$ _____ **15.** $3.7 + 4.2 =$ _____

Solve.

16. Mrs. Chehval drives 5.2 miles to work, 1.7 miles to the store, and 6.7 miles home. How many miles does she drive?

17. Terry rides his bike to deliver papers. He rides 0.5 miles on one street and 1.4 miles on another. How many miles does Terry ride?

_____

_____

Mixed Review

Add, subtract, multiply, or divide.

1. $\begin{array}{r}48\\+73\\\hline\end{array}$	**2.** $\begin{array}{r}174\\+259\\\hline\end{array}$	**3.** $\begin{array}{r}213\\+176\\\hline\end{array}$	**4.** $\begin{array}{r}433\\-189\\\hline\end{array}$
5. $\begin{array}{r}218\\-172\\\hline\end{array}$	**6.** $\begin{array}{r}527\\-219\\\hline\end{array}$	**7.** $\begin{array}{r}8\\\times 8\\\hline\end{array}$	**8.** $\begin{array}{r}7\\\times 8\\\hline\end{array}$

9. $8 \times 8 =$ _____ **10.** $8\overline{)72}$ **11.** $8\overline{)48}$ **12.** $8\overline{)40}$

Use with text pages 388–389.

Subtracting with Decimals

Subtract.

1. $\begin{array}{r} 0.9 \\ -0.7 \\ \hline \end{array}$ 2. $\begin{array}{r} 0.6 \\ -0.2 \\ \hline \end{array}$ 3. $\begin{array}{r} 0.4 \\ -0.3 \\ \hline \end{array}$ 4. $\begin{array}{r} 1.2 \\ -0.6 \\ \hline \end{array}$

5. $\begin{array}{r} 1.1 \\ -1.1 \\ \hline \end{array}$ 6. $\begin{array}{r} 1.1 \\ -0.9 \\ \hline \end{array}$ 7. $\begin{array}{r} 3.1 \\ -2.5 \\ \hline \end{array}$ 8. $\begin{array}{r} 4.6 \\ -0.9 \\ \hline \end{array}$

9. $\begin{array}{r} 4.8 \\ -3.5 \\ \hline \end{array}$ 10. $\begin{array}{r} 2.7 \\ -1.4 \\ \hline \end{array}$ 11. $\begin{array}{r} 6.5 \\ -4.9 \\ \hline \end{array}$ 12. $\begin{array}{r} 6.3 \\ -1.8 \\ \hline \end{array}$

13. $\begin{array}{r} 7.5 \\ -2.1 \\ \hline \end{array}$ 14. $\begin{array}{r} 6.3 \\ -1.8 \\ \hline \end{array}$ 15. $\begin{array}{r} 9.5 \\ -2.7 \\ \hline \end{array}$ 16. $\begin{array}{r} 5.8 \\ -2.1 \\ \hline \end{array}$

17. $9.7 - 5.2 = $ _____   18. $3.6 - 1.2 = $ _____

19. $8.2 - 5.6 = $ _____   20. $7.1 - 3.2 = $ _____

Mixed Review

Add, subtract, multiply, or divide.

1. $\begin{array}{r} 6 \\ 2 \\ +9 \\ \hline \end{array}$ 2. $\begin{array}{r} 4 \\ 5 \\ +3 \\ \hline \end{array}$ 3. $\begin{array}{r} 3 \\ 4 \\ +7 \\ \hline \end{array}$ 4. $\begin{array}{r} 6,745 \\ -4,123 \\ \hline \end{array}$

5. $\begin{array}{r} 9,847 \\ -3,216 \\ \hline \end{array}$ 6. $\begin{array}{r} 6,864 \\ -4,012 \\ \hline \end{array}$ 7. $\begin{array}{r} 9 \\ \times 7 \\ \hline \end{array}$ 8. $\begin{array}{r} 6 \\ \times 7 \\ \hline \end{array}$

9. $8 \times 7 = $ ___   10. $7\overline{)28}$ 11. $7\overline{)49}$ 12. $7\overline{)21}$

Use with text pages 396–397.

Using Patterns to Multiply Tens

Use patterns to find the products mentally.

1. $\begin{array}{r} 1 \\ \times 4 \\ \hline \end{array}$ $\begin{array}{r} 10 \\ \times\ 4 \\ \hline \end{array}$ **2.** $\begin{array}{r} 1 \\ \times 5 \\ \hline \end{array}$ $\begin{array}{r} 10 \\ \times\ 5 \\ \hline \end{array}$ **3.** $\begin{array}{r} 1 \\ \times 6 \\ \hline \end{array}$ $\begin{array}{r} 10 \\ \times\ 6 \\ \hline \end{array}$

4. $\begin{array}{r} 1 \\ \times 7 \\ \hline \end{array}$ $\begin{array}{r} 10 \\ \times\ 7 \\ \hline \end{array}$ **5.** $\begin{array}{r} 1 \\ \times 8 \\ \hline \end{array}$ $\begin{array}{r} 10 \\ \times\ 8 \\ \hline \end{array}$ **6.** $\begin{array}{r} 1 \\ \times 9 \\ \hline \end{array}$ $\begin{array}{r} 10 \\ \times\ 9 \\ \hline \end{array}$

7. $\begin{array}{r} 2 \\ \times 2 \\ \hline \end{array}$ $\begin{array}{r} 20 \\ \times\ 2 \\ \hline \end{array}$ **8.** $\begin{array}{r} 2 \\ \times 3 \\ \hline \end{array}$ $\begin{array}{r} 20 \\ \times\ 3 \\ \hline \end{array}$ **9.** $\begin{array}{r} 2 \\ \times 4 \\ \hline \end{array}$ $\begin{array}{r} 20 \\ \times\ 4 \\ \hline \end{array}$

10. $\begin{array}{r} 7 \\ \times 3 \\ \hline \end{array}$ $\begin{array}{r} 70 \\ \times\ 3 \\ \hline \end{array}$ **11.** $\begin{array}{r} 5 \\ \times 4 \\ \hline \end{array}$ $\begin{array}{r} 50 \\ \times\ 4 \\ \hline \end{array}$ **12.** $\begin{array}{r} 6 \\ \times 8 \\ \hline \end{array}$ $\begin{array}{r} 60 \\ \times\ 8 \\ \hline \end{array}$

13. $4 \times 3 =$ _____   **14.** $9 \times 2 =$ _____   **15.** $8 \times 7 =$ _____

$40 \times 3 =$ _____ $90 \times 2 =$ _____ $80 \times 7 =$ _____

Mixed Review

Add, subtract, multiply, or divide.

1. $\begin{array}{r} 8 \\ +4 \\ \hline \end{array}$ **2.** $\begin{array}{r} 8 \\ -4 \\ \hline \end{array}$ **3.** $\begin{array}{r} 8 \\ \times 4 \\ \hline \end{array}$ **4.** $4\overline{)8}$

5. $\begin{array}{r} 9 \\ +9 \\ \hline \end{array}$ **6.** $\begin{array}{r} 9 \\ \times 9 \\ \hline \end{array}$ **7.** $\begin{array}{r} 9 \\ -9 \\ \hline \end{array}$ **8.** $9\overline{)9}$

Using Patterns to Multiply Hundreds

Use patterns to multiply mentally.

1.
$$\begin{array}{r} 1 \\ \times 5 \end{array} \quad \begin{array}{r} 10 \\ \times 5 \end{array} \quad \begin{array}{r} 100 \\ \times 5 \end{array}$$

2.
$$\begin{array}{r} 3 \\ \times 4 \end{array} \quad \begin{array}{r} 30 \\ \times 4 \end{array} \quad \begin{array}{r} 300 \\ \times 4 \end{array}$$

3.
$$\begin{array}{r} 2 \\ \times 6 \end{array} \quad \begin{array}{r} 20 \\ \times 6 \end{array} \quad \begin{array}{r} 200 \\ \times 6 \end{array}$$

4.
$$\begin{array}{r} 6 \\ \times 8 \end{array} \quad \begin{array}{r} 60 \\ \times 8 \end{array} \quad \begin{array}{r} 600 \\ \times 8 \end{array}$$

5.
$$\begin{array}{r} 4 \\ \times 7 \end{array} \quad \begin{array}{r} 40 \\ \times 7 \end{array} \quad \begin{array}{r} 400 \\ \times 7 \end{array}$$

6.
$$\begin{array}{r} 7 \\ \times 9 \end{array} \quad \begin{array}{r} 70 \\ \times 9 \end{array} \quad \begin{array}{r} 700 \\ \times 9 \end{array}$$

7. $3 \times 100 =$ _____   8. $4 \times 200 =$ _____   9. $2 \times 300 =$ _____

10. $5 \times 200 =$ _____   11. $4 \times 300 =$ _____   12. $6 \times 200 =$ _____

13. $5 \times 700 =$ _____   14. $6 \times 400 =$ _____   15. $7 \times 300 =$ _____

Mixed Review

Write the decimal for each.

1. nine and six tenths _____

2. $8\frac{79}{100}$ _____

3. ninety-six hundredths _____

4. $3\frac{1}{10}$ _____

5. nine and six hundredths _____

6. $\frac{9}{100}$ _____

Multiplying a Two-Digit Number by a One-Digit Number

Multiply. Use base-ten blocks if you like.

1. 12×4

2. 23×3

3. 15×6

4. 44×2

5. 26×5

6. 43×5

7. 64×2

8. 37×5

9. 54×8

10. 69×7

11. 74×6

12. 39×9

13. $62 \times 4 =$ _____

14. $27 \times 2 =$ _____

15. $29 \times 6 =$ _____

16. $35 \times 5 =$ _____

17. $43 \times 3 =$ _____

18. $62 \times 7 =$ _____

19. $81 \times 6 =$ _____

20. $32 \times 7 =$ _____

21. $59 \times 3 =$ _____

Find each missing digit.

22. $3\square \times 2 = 72$

23. $1\square \times 7 = 98$

24. $28 \times \square = 84$

25. $37 \times \square = 74$

Mixed Review

◆ Add, subtract, or multiply. Use mental math or paper and pencil.

1. $4.5 + 2.1$

2. $0.7 + 0.8$

3. $0.3 + 0.4$

4. $0.9 - 0.2$

5. $1.3 - 0.4$

6. $3.2 - 1.7$

7. 5×4

8. 6×5

© Silver, Burdett & Ginn Inc.

Name _____

Use with text pages 406–407.

Estimating Products

Estimate each product.

1. 72	2. 38	3. 93	4. 66
× 3	× 4	× 7	× 3

5. 377	6. 213	7. 623	8. 782
× 6	× 8	× 2	× 7

9. $7 \times 78 =$ _____   10. $5 \times 495 =$ _____   11. $3 \times 828 =$ _____

Estimate. Write $>$, $<$, or $=$ in each $\bigcirc$.

12. $7 \times 38 \bigcirc 300$

13. $40 \times 6 \bigcirc 8 \times 30$

14. $6 \times 71 \bigcirc 49 \times 8$

15. $120 \times 7 \bigcirc 2 \times 308$

Use estimation to solve.

16. Lorna is making jewelry. Each necklace has 8 beads. About how many beads does she need to make 27 necklaces.   _____ beads

17. Theo has 23 math problems for homework each night. About how many problems does he have in 7 nights?   _____ problems

Mixed Review

Add, subtract, multiply, or divide.

1. 6.4	2. 2.4	3. 4.7	4. 3.8
+2.8	−1.5	+3.7	−2.2

5. 8	6. 5	7. 6	8. 12
×6	×7	×4	× 0

9. $2\overline{)16}$ 10. $7\overline{)21}$ 11. $3\overline{)24}$ 12. $8\overline{)40}$

Use with text pages 408–409.

Multiplying Three-Digit Numbers

Multiply.

1. 222
   × 4

2. 142
   × 2

3. 101
   × 8

4. 103
   × 3

5. 210
   × 3

6. 105
   × 8

7. 106
   × 9

8. 108
   × 7

9. 112
   × 7

10. 115
    × 5

11. 120
    × 6

12. 121
    × 6

13. 140
    × 5

14. 141
    × 5

15. 162
    × 4

16. 412
    × 6

17. 500
    × 6

18. 580
    × 4

19. 900
    × 9

20. 400
    × 7

21. 401
    × 4

22. 517
    × 5

23. 327
    × 3

24. 202
    × 8

25. 900
    × 0

Mixed Review

Name each figure.

1. four equal straight sides _____

2. no straight sides and no corners _____

3. three straight sides and three corners _____

4.

5.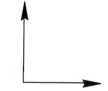

6.

_____   _____   _____

Use with text pages 403–409.

Multiplying Greater Numbers

Ring the better estimate.

1. 409 × 6

240 or 2,400

2. 598 × 7

3,500 or 4,200

3. 920 × 5

4,500 or 5,300

Estimate. Then find each product.

4. 615
× 7

5. 921
× 8

6. 785
× 7

7. 510
× 6

8. 499
× 5

9. 509
× 7

10. 514
× 6

11. 620
× 8

12. 732
× 3

13. 715
× 9

14. 681
× 6

15. 823
× 8

Mixed Review

Find the perimeter of each figure.

1.

3 cm
3 cm

_____

2.
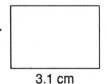
2.7 cm
3.1 cm

_____

3.
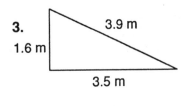
3.9 m
1.6 m
3.5 m

_____

Problem-Solving Strategies: Logic

1. A farmer has 3 fields of different sizes for his crops. His plan is to plant more corn than soybeans and more soybeans than spinach. What should he plant in

   field A? _____

   field B? _____

   field C? _____

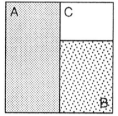

2. Tom is older than Bob.

   Mary is younger than Susan.

   Bob is older than Mary.

   Susan is older than Tom.

   List the names according to age, starting with the youngest.

   _____   _____   _____   _____

Mixed Strategy Review

1. Use the drawing above to list the fields by letter from largest to smallest.

   _____   _____   _____

Add or subtract.

2. 237
   +869

3. 791
   −609

4. 3,685
   −2,087

5. 9,679
   + 843

Use with text pages 416–417.

Using Patterns to Divide Tens and Hundreds

Use patterns to divide.

1. $2\overline{)4}$ $2\overline{)40}$ $2\overline{)400}$ 2. $4\overline{)24}$ $4\overline{)240}$ $4\overline{)2,400}$

3. $5\overline{)35}$ $5\overline{)350}$ $5\overline{)3,500}$ 4. $7\overline{)21}$ $7\overline{)210}$ $7\overline{)2,100}$

5. $3\overline{)27}$ $3\overline{)270}$ $3\overline{)2,700}$ 6. $6\overline{)30}$ $6\overline{)300}$ $6\overline{)3,000}$

7. $3\overline{)900}$ 8. $8\overline{)3,200}$ 9. $6\overline{)4,800}$

10. $350 \div 5 =$ _____   11. $1,500 \div 3 =$ _____   12. $1,600 \div 8 =$ _____

Find each missing number.

13. $8 \div$ _____ $= 1$ 14. $80 \div$ _____ $= 10$ 15. $800 \div$ ____ $= 100$

Solve.

16. There are 60 third graders in Park School. There are the same number of students in each of the 3 classrooms. How many third graders are in each room?   _____ third graders

17. There are 150 dirty desks. Five students offer to wash them. How many desks will each students wash if each student washes the same number of desks?   _____ desks

---

Mixed Review

Add or subtract.

1. $\begin{array}{r} 345 \\ +534 \end{array}$ 2. $\begin{array}{r} 198 \\ +764 \end{array}$ 3. $\begin{array}{r} 549 \\ +429 \end{array}$ 4. $\begin{array}{r} 397 \\ -218 \end{array}$ 5. $\begin{array}{r} 617 \\ -338 \end{array}$ 6. $\begin{array}{r} 645 \\ -223 \end{array}$

Use with text pages 416–423.

Dividing by One-Digit Numbers

Find each quotient.

1. $2\overline{)16}$ 2. $5\overline{)18}$ 3. $4\overline{)29}$ 4. $5\overline{)27}$

5. $6\overline{)62}$ 6. $5\overline{)60}$ 7. $5\overline{)86}$ 8. $4\overline{)87}$

9. $78 \div 7 =$ _____   10. $84 \div 9 =$ _____   11. $72 \div 8 =$ _____

12. $76 \div 5 =$ _____   13. $95 \div 3 =$ _____   14. $87 \div 2 =$ _____

Compare. Write >, <, or = in each ◯.

15. $90 \div 3 \bigcirc 90 \div 4$ 16. $38 \div 4 \bigcirc 29 \div 3$

17. $96 \div 3 \bigcirc 16 \times 2$ 18. $47 \div 6 \bigcirc 53 \div 8$

19. $31 \div 3 \bigcirc 43 \div 4$ 20. $50 \div 7 \bigcirc 60 \div 8$

Mixed Review

◆ Add, subtract, multiply, or divide.
Use mental math or paper and pencil.

1. $\begin{array}{r} 378 \\ +287 \\ \hline \end{array}$ 2. $\begin{array}{r} 429 \\ -197 \\ \hline \end{array}$ 3. $\begin{array}{r} 335 \\ +479 \\ \hline \end{array}$ 4. $\begin{array}{r} 8,674 \\ -3,012 \\ \hline \end{array}$ 5. $\begin{array}{r} 72 \\ \times 6 \\ \hline \end{array}$

6. $210 \times 0 =$ _____   7. $9\overline{)0}$ 8. $6\overline{)48}$ 9. $49 \div 7 =$ _____

Name _____

Review 1

Add or subtract.

1. 37	2. 56	3. 216	4. 119	5. 442	6. 530
−19	+98	− 77	−119	+329	−215

7. $68 + 11 + 24 =$ _____   8. $28 + 33 + 58 =$ _____   9. $12 + 47 + 26 =$ _____

10. $757 − 246 =$ _____   11. $360 − 148 =$ _____   12. $353 − 85 =$ _____

Estimate. Then find each sum or difference.

13. 32	14. 48	15. 31	16. 416	17. 723	18. 400
−18	−39	+19	+321	−303	−209

Write each number in standard form.

19. six thousand, two hundred fifteen _____

20. ninety-two thousand, four hundred _____

21. forty thousand, three hundred eleven _____

Compare. Write $>$, $<$, or $=$ in each $\bigcirc$.

22. 4,801 $\bigcirc$ 4,810   23. 32,380 $\bigcirc$ 32,000

24. 432 + 213 $\bigcirc$ 45 + 563   25. 432 − 87 $\bigcirc$ 255 + 90

Solve.

26. Mrs. Carlson had $4,562 in her bank
account. She added $589 to the account.
How much money does she have now? _____

Review 2

Write the time.

1. It is 12:15 P.M. Lunch starts in 15 minutes. What time does lunch start?

_____

2. It is 11:30 A.M. What time will it be in 1 hour and 40 minutes?

_____

Use the graph.

3. What are the coordinates of point A?

_____

4. Locate the following points on the graph and label.
   B (6,8) and C (3,4)

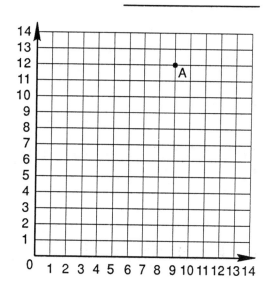

Multiply.

5. $\begin{array}{r} 8 \\ \times 4 \\ \hline \end{array}$

6. $\begin{array}{r} 5 \\ \times 7 \\ \hline \end{array}$

7. $\begin{array}{r} 4 \\ \times 3 \\ \hline \end{array}$

8. $\begin{array}{r} 9 \\ \times 8 \\ \hline \end{array}$

9. $\begin{array}{r} 7 \\ \times 6 \\ \hline \end{array}$

10. $\begin{array}{r} 6 \\ \times 3 \\ \hline \end{array}$

11. $\begin{array}{r} 8 \\ \times 7 \\ \hline \end{array}$

12. $0 \times 5 =$ _____

13. $5 \times 9 =$ _____

14. $6 \times 6 =$ _____

15. $3 \times 2 \times 6 =$ _____

16. $2 \times 2 \times 7 =$ _____

17. $4 \times 1 \times 9 =$ _____

Use the bar graph.

18. Complete the graph to show that 7 students chose chicken nuggets as their favorite lunch.

19. Which lunch did 4 students choose as their favorite?

_____

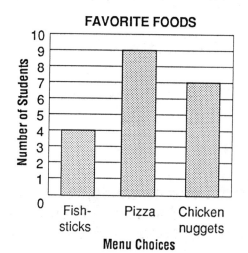

Name _____

Review 3

Find each quotient.

1. 10 ÷ 2 = _____   **2.** 16 ÷ 4 = _____   **3.** 18 ÷ 3 = _____

4. 1)‾6   **5.** 7)‾0   **6.** 8)‾48   **7.** 5)‾45

Complete each fact family.

8. 7 × 6 = 42   _____   **9.** 40 ÷ 8 = 5   _____

_____   _____   _____   _____

Write a fraction or mixed number for the shaded parts.

10.   **11.** 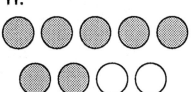   **12.**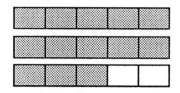

____   ____   ____

Complete.

13. $\frac{1}{5}$ of 30 = ____   **14.** $\frac{1}{7}$ of 63 = ____   **15.** $\frac{1}{3}$ of 21 = ____

Compare. Write >, <, or = in each ◯.

16. $\frac{2}{5}$ ◯ $\frac{4}{5}$ **17.** $\frac{1}{6}$ ◯ $\frac{1}{9}$ **18.** $\frac{3}{6}$ ◯ $\frac{1}{2}$

Ring the better estimate for each.

19. height of a house   **20.** full pitcher of water

5 km   or   5 m   2 pints   or   2 gallons

Name _____

Review 4

Name each figure.

1.   2.   3.   4.

_____   _____   _____   _____

Find the perimeter.   Find the area.

5.

2 cm

4 cm

perimeter = _____ cm

6.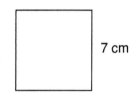

7 cm

area = _____ cm²

Write a fraction and a decimal for each shaded region.

7. 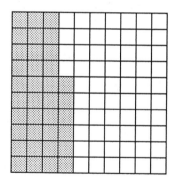   _____

_____

8.    _____

_____

Estimate. Then find each product.

9. 235
   × 6

10. 678
    × 4

11. 508
    × 2

12. 698
    × 5

Divide.

13. 7)350   14. 4)8,000   15. 6)4,200

Problem-Solving Review

Library		
Opens 7:50 A.M.		Math book $3.95
Closes 3:45 P.M.	**Bookstore**	Science book . . . $3.95
Return books by	Opens 8:00 A.M.	Notebook 39
3:30 P.M.	Closes 4:00 P.M.	Pencil 25
		Pen 17

Cross out any extra information.
Use the signs to solve.

1. Connie has $5. Can she buy a new math
   book and a pencil. _____

2. Jeremy arrived at school at 7:45. How long
   will he have to wait for the library to open? _____

3. Mrs. Petrie works in the bookstore. Miss
   Gallen works in the cafeteria. How long
   does Mrs. Petrie work each day if she has a
   30 minute lunch? _____

4. Timmy had 60¢. He bought 2 items at the
   bookstore. What possible items could he _____
   buy? _____

5. Emily begins putting books on the shelves
   at 3:30. Emily can shelf 2 books every
   minute. How many books will Emily put on
   the shelves by the time the library closes? _____

Choose the missing information. Then solve.

6. Pamela bought a new pen. How much
   change did she receive?

   a. Pamela arrived at school at 7:40.

   b. Pamela had 25¢.

   c. Pamela lost her math book. _____